What's Up?

Activities for Responding to Children's Lives

E. Sandy Powell

THOMSON
✳
DELMAR LEARNING

Australia Canada Mexico Singapore Spain United Kingdom United States

THOMSON

DELMAR LEARNING

What's Up?:
Activities for Responding to Children's Lives
E. Sandy Powell

Business Unit Executive Director: Susan L. Simpfenderfer	**Executive Production Manager:** Wendy A. Troeger	**Executive Marketing Manager:** Donna J. Lewis
Acquisitions Editor: Erin O'Connor Traylor	**Production Editor:** J.P. Henkel	**Channel Manager:** Nigar Hale
Editorial Assistant: Ivy Ip	**Technology Project Manager:** Joe Saba	**Cover Design:** Tom Cicero

COPYRIGHT © 2003 E. Sandy Powell.

Printed in the United States
1 2 3 4 5 GP 06 05 04 03 02

For more information, contact Delmar Learning, 5 Maxwell Drive, Clifton Park, NY 12065-2919

Or you can visit our Internet site at http://www.delmarlearning.com

Library of Congress Cataloging-in-Publication Data
Powell, E. Sandy
   What's up?: activities for responding to children's lives/ E. Sandy Powell.—1st ed.
      p. cm.
   ISBN 1-40181-587-1
      1. Early childhood education—Activity programs. I. Title.

LB1139.35.A37 P69 2002
372.21—dc21   2002035046

NOTICE TO THE READER

What's Up? is dedicated
to the memory of my mom, Kay Powell,
who is so present in this work
and in the lives of her children,
grandchildren, and great-grandchildren,
and to my dad, Ken Powell,
who is, thankfully, always involved
in whatever's up
in our lives.

Table of Contents

Preface   vi
About the Author   xi
Acknowledgments   xii
Avenue for Feedback   xiv

Introduction   1

Family Play   6

To the **Beach**, 7
On a **Bus Ride**, 12
Into a **Butterfly Garden**, 17
On a **Camping Trip**, 22
On a **Car Trip**, 26
Into a **Cave**, 31
Going **Fishing**, 37
To a **Horse Ranch**, 43
At the **Laundromat**, 49
To the **Park**, 53
To a **Pet Store**, 58
To a **Pond**, 63
Reading on a Blanket, under the Apple Tree, 66
To the **Woods**, 71
In the **Yard**, (to Watch a Worm), 76
To the **Zoo**, 80

Family Work   83

Artist, 84
Astronaut, 89
Baker, 94
City Planner, 99
Construction Worker, 103
Farmer, 108
Fast Food Service Worker, 112
Firefighter, 116

Garbage Collector/Recycler, 121
Hair Stylist, 126
Holistic Health Worker, 129
Homemaker, 135
House Painter, 140
Inventor, 143
Laboratory Scientist, 148
Librarian, 152
Mechanic, 157
Naturalist, 161
Pilot, 166
Police Officer, 171
Postal Worker, 175
Real Estate Salesperson, 179
Scuba Diver, 183
Used Car Salesperson, 185
Weather Forecaster, 188
Web Page Designer, 192
Window Washer, 196

Changes   199

Car **Accident**, 202
New **Baby**, 207
Family Member's **Birthday**, 213
Caring for an Aging Adult, 216
First **Cold Spell** of the Year, 222
Death of a Family Member, 226
Becoming **Differently-Abled**, 233
Divorce, 237
Drug and Alcohol Abuse, 243
Fire, 245
Friend or Sibling **Good-bye**, 248
Parent's **Hospital Stay**, 252
Moving, 256
Birth or Acquisition of a **Pet**, 261
Parent's **Remarriage**, 266
Home Repair or **Remodeling**, 270
Change in **Teacher or Caregiver**, 275
Terminal Illness in the Family, 280
Parent **Traveling**, 283
Tumultuous Times, 286
Family **Violence**, 290

In Closing   294

Appendix   295

Recycled Materials to Have on Hand, 295
Supplies to Have on Hand, 295
Expand on the Topics with Flannel Board Activities, 295
Winger Puppet Pattern, 298
Song Sheets, 302
Premade Books, 303
Home Involvement, 303

Preface

As a founding child care center director, and especially as a home caregiver, I was able to respond to each child as a unique individual whose interests and matters of the heart were every bit as important as prescribed early learning concepts. In my five years as a home child care provider, I was continually spinning our activities out of the children's real interests and creating experiences as an outcome of what I called our "group myth."

When working as a teacher, though, in early childhood settings, I often felt frustrated. It was difficult to respond to individual needs and interests while trying to meet the required curriculum guidelines. I noticed other teachers similarly stymied. We would work ourselves to exhaustion, racing to the library for follow-up songs, stories, etc., or shopping for necessary materials to adapt elaborate projects gleaned from any number of activity books, yet we would often be missing direct response to the children. I couldn't ignore what was up in a child's life, especially the traumatic changes such as an apartment fire, a grandmother's death, the babysitter's goodbye, a parent's hospital stay. I began to think there should be some tool to enable teachers to easily respond to individual children's lives. I wanted specific activities for the clinging boy whose social interactions were impeded by the threat of divorce or the girl whose mother worked so valiantly, yet with little or no money, to provide rich experiences for her daughter.

Field Study Results:

So I took my idea to Head Start teachers in our area. They cheered the concept, offering detailed criterion for what would be useful. Then I took their ideas to public kindergarten through second grade teachers, private preschool teachers, and child care providers. Unanimously, the teachers agreed that an activities book that could help them respond to individual children's lives has been needed for years, now more than ever as the infrastructures of family and society dramatically change. The more acknowledged and heard a child feels, the better able she is to attend to learning of any kind. But the teachers said it didn't matter how much good the activities would do, the individualizing concept would be worthless if they had to search, research, shop, or plan in-depth. Teachers and caregivers just don't have time. Here's what was wanted:

activities from on-hand, largely recycled materials
self-contained ideas
highlighted tasks for ease in delegating to aides or parent helpers
activities children really enjoy
ways to address the child's whole development
ideas that take little or no prep-time, including to-the-point
instructions, without wordy rationale
activities that target a cross-section of population, not just the
economically advantaged.

I wrote *What's Up?* for these teachers and caregivers, and ultimately for their children who deserve to be heard and validated.

The Markets for Which This Book Is Specially Geared:

What's Up? offers enrichment activities sought by many groups: preschools, Head Start, child care centers, Early Childhood Education divisions of public and private schools, home child care programs, play therapy units, parents, grandparents, or any adults seeking affirming activities for their young children. Teacher training programs may be especially interested in this approach to building self-esteem.

The Teacher-Friendly Mechanics of the Book:

The teacher will have at-the-ready, a range of individualizing activities, with options available for matching a child's particular learning style or addressing the need for specific skill development. Teachers can easily adapt and create their own activities, using this extensive set as a core model.

Teachers may also have their own favorite curriculum item to supplement a particular section in *What's Up?* I realize early childhood folks are in and out of the library on a regular basis. For these activities, though, a teacher won't *have* to search out connected pieces from several different resources. Complete sets of activities and literature for responding to an event or interest in a child's home life are contained within *What's Up?*

At a glance, teachers can spot the different kinds of activities by their identifying tabs. The set-up tasks, which can be completed by parent helpers or volunteers, are also marked for easy identification.

Link to Early Childhood Pioneer, Lucy Sprague Mitchell:

In the pioneering tradition of Lucy Sprague Mitchell's *Here and Now Story Book,* the vignettes in *What's Up?* speak directly to the children about interests and events in their daily lives. The language is of the child, addressing whatever is "up" at any give time. I have bent my intention towards writing literature, with cadence and spirit worthy of precious early learners, while still meeting the applicability needs of their teachers. Lucy Sprague Mitchell, founder of Bank Street College, first gave us this model of integrating actual events in children's lives into real literature. Lucy, Harriet Johnson, and Caroline Pratt then laid the groundwork for combining stories with interdisciplinary activities that touched the children in their care.

Three characters emerged during my writing to facilitate this kind of interaction with children. Winger, Skippety, and Weaver Finch offer musings, poems, and stories to help handle the challenges that arise while working with young children and families. The characters also bring life and spark when the teacher is over-extended or tired. If you ask child therapists, they will recognize the characters as essential archetypal figures in a healthily developing child's life. If you show the characters to children, they will want to interact with Winger, Skippety, and Weaver Finch; the characters speak their language and touch their hearts. And finally, if you ask early childhood teachers, they will sound relieved to be able to rely on trusted "friends" for words to begin conversations when events such as death or accident strikes.

Linking children's home and school selves may be even more important now in our speeded-up society, where children are shuttled from one scheduled event to another, often from one part of their family to another. *What's Up?* is an outgrowth of our foremothers' work, as it provides, in a teacher-friendly format, activities for utilizing their innovations effectively in the twenty-first century.

The Individualizing Approach:

This is a book of validation. It is full of activities that authenticate children's feelings, their perspective, and a lot of their life experience.

This is not meant to be a book that *teaches* about professions, although children will learn as they hear the names for real jobs, tools, and work activities. It is a book that will help children grow in all areas of their development, through activities about work that matter in their families' lives.

This book is not meant to provide family vacation plans either, or to *teach* how to be with one's children. Admittedly, the activities reflect a valuing of simple experiences, as compared to those that cost money, especially a great deal of money. The bias is intentional, hoping in one small way to help right the imbalance between the have's and have-not's in our society. These activities honor parent/child relationships, regardless of financial standing. These are types of playing all families have done, or could enjoy doing, together.

Neither is this book meant to *teach* children how to process changes in their lives. It is meant to acknowledge and accept that children *are* processing changes constantly, sometimes working through great distress. This book encourages teachers to give children space and time to do so in acceptable ways.

The activities are age-appropriate, and developmentally sound. Hopefully, school and child care administrators will realize that any time taken away from the regular curriculum is time well-spent because the objectives are consistent with a wide spectrum of early childhood philosophies. The activities can enhance any classroom, fitting into lulls in the weekly schedule, or into slots in the daily routine, such as "circle time" activities or "station" choices. The teacher has the freedom to adapt the activities to fit his unique teaching style.

Since the overall intent of *What's Up?* is to spur individualizing curriculum, the activities will work for a wide age range, from young preschoolers through early elementary school. Teachers may need to adapt some activities to fit their children's specific developmental needs. Not all of the activities in this book are meant for all children. For instance, teachers of younger preschool children may find some of the game directions too complicated. In that case, the teacher can skip the game and use the story telling or project in that section instead. The variety of activities provide teachers with options in each topic to meet the individual and group needs in a positive and safe manner.

Common sense should always accompany your use of the activities. When in doubt about the appropriateness of an activity for a particular child or group, consult your school or center's director, or an available professional service such as a Child Care Resource and Referral organization, before presenting it to your children. As author I support the use of safety practices suited to your situation. Do not abandon good judgment.

You may not be able to introduce some activities to your children because of their individual needs or because of your facility's particular physical limitations. For instance, you may have children with allergies who are unable to eat certain food items presented in this book. Likewise, you may be caring for children who aren't developmentally able to keep small items out of their mouths, even though others in the group are trustworthy with tiny objects. Teachers may need to adapt an art project, eliminating the smaller items, or having children tear paper if they aren't yet able to manipulate scissors, or *slice bananas* with a table knife, rather than *chopping vegetables.* Adapt the activities whenever necessary, keeping the children's physical safety and emotional well-being your primary considerations.

I have alternated gender references equally throughout, sometimes referring to a child or teacher as she, sometimes as he, to maintain equitability while allowing the words to flow freely. All activities and references are intended for both genders.

I recognize that it's hard for teachers to consider implementing yet one more strategy. The trade-off for providing individualized activities will be improvement in the children's behaviors and a rise in their self-esteem. As a bonus, responding to children individually provides teacher satisfaction at the soul level. This book was created in response to real children. I hope you can use it joyfully with yours.

Online Resources

Visit www.earlychilded.delmar.com to access Online Resources related to *What's Up?*

About the Author

E. Sandy Powell comes to us as writer, mother, brand-new grandma, teacher, and learner. She leaves none of these behind as she listens to children, creating an individualizing activities collection that will enable early childhood professionals to validate "whatever's up" in a child's life.

Ms. Powell received the City University Board of Governor's merit scholarship to complete her Master's in Education at age 49. She earned her degree magna cum laude, with emphasis on Curriculum and Instruction. Ms. Powell spent 15 years in Early Childhood Education, teaching in various early learning settings, founding and directing child care centers, coordinating before and after school programs in the public schools, running her own home child care business for five years, and homeschooling her children for a number of their school grades. She also taught Adult Basic Education at Clark College for five years, and taught Women's Studies for one quarter, also at Clark. Sandy now uses her heart-centered teaching skills on the Southern Oregon Coast. She teaches Adult Basic Education and English as a Second Language at one of Southwestern Oregon Community College's branch sites. She's tickled, too, to have brought an Introduction to Women's Studies course to the Southern Oregon Coast. Known to kids as "Sparky," Ms. Powell keeps in touch with children and their curriculum needs by substitute teaching in two school districts, grades K–12. She is a member of the National Association for the Education of Young Children (NAEYC), and the American Association for Women in Community Colleges (AAWCC).

E. Sandy Powell has authored six other books, five of them for children, three of those on tough subjects: bereavement, abuse, and homelessness. *Daisy* was chosen by the National Council on Social Studies and the Children' Book Council. Ms. Powell has completed a college textbook, as yet unpublished, on our mighty foremothers in education. She smiles at the remembrance of having written her first book, *Heart to Heart Caregiving,* with children all about, much like many of our foremothers.

Acknowledgments

My three grown children and their families inspire and nurture me through these writing projects, each in their own special way. I am ever so thankful for their involvement in my writing life. In this book, thanks is due my youngest daughter for granting me use of her imaginary childhood friend, Winger. And to countless other family and friends for their steady encouragement.

I am grateful to the many adults, especially Connie, from whom I have learned how to sit with a child's pain, as much as with a child's joy. Life holds all.

I wholeheartedly thank Acquisitions Editor Erin O'Connor for her steadfast belief in the work. I also appreciate the folks at Delmar Learning and Carlisle Publishers Services who helped to bring *What's Up?* into your schools and childcare centers.

I appreciate the reviewers enlisted through Delmar for their constructive criticism and helpful suggestions. They include:

Jennifer Berke, PhD
Mercyhurst College–North East
North East, PA

Wendy Bertoli
Lancaster County Career and Technology Center
Lancaster, PA

Jody Martin
Children's World Learning Centers
Golden, CO

Vicki Milstein
Early Childhood Coordinator
Brookline Public Schools
Brookline, MA

Brenda Schin
Child Care Provider
Selkirk, NY

Thank you.

Finally, I remember and credit each and every child who has come into my life over the years. The children made clear their need to be heard, so this book is really from them.

Avenue for Feedback

The author can be contacted at

E. Sandy Powell, Author
c/o Erin O'Connor
Thomson/Delmar Learning
Executive Woods
5 Maxwell Drive
Clifton Park, NY 12065-2919.

I will be happy to hear how the activities have worked for your children. Also, if you have any thoughts on activities that you'd like to offer for subsequent books, we'll welcome your ideas. Please share original ideas only, not those found in other texts.

Thanks ahead of time. I look forward to hearing from you.

Under bright sky,

E. Sandy Powell

Introduction

Children come to us full of life. Even at three and four years old they have deeply felt interests and their own particular ways of doing things. Applauding uniqueness and nurturing self-esteem have become primary goals among teachers of young children. Without a positive image of self, learning is hampered and healthy interactions threatened.

Sometimes though, for whatever reasons, a school will compile a set of objectives, perhaps ones that meet parents' expectations for early academics. Tending to these objectives can end up requiring all of a teacher's time and focus. Consequently, those bubbling, effervescing youngsters have to check their personal interests, their family challenges, and empowering strengths at the door, tucking their home-selves into a cubby, along with their toys and snips of blankie. Presumably, the teacher can then "teach" the curriculum. But no children come to us blank. Even if we require them to leave the trappings of home at home, they still arrive, full of the richest, sometimes turbulent, life experiences, which naturally overflow into their time in the group.

For all of you who hold dear the preciousness of each individual child, this book can bridge children's home and school/child care lives. You will find quick and easy ways to respond to important particulars in each child's life. You will be able to choose from activities that suit your children, and fit those activities smoothly into whatever system your school or child care center endorses.

Be sure to adapt any of the activities, such as the stretching exercises in the Family Work, Holistic Health section, to suit children who are differently-abled. You will know, from your close association, what each child can and cannot do. Use these as a beginning point for activities that truly match your children.

This book makes individualizing curriculum easy. The activities are contained right here. There's no searching in libraries or on other teachers' shelves, frantically hoping to find a story or song that corresponds with the topic. Since most teachers have precious little prep time, everything from children's literature to outdoor games, imaginative play set-up instructions to cooperative sculpting experiences are all right here. Activities help in large and small muscle development, social interaction, self-esteem building, and language acquisition. You'll find projects, games, and experiments relating to traditional art, music, pre-science, and math programs, all interwoven in an interdisciplinary format appropriate for children in early childhood.

And you won't need to go shopping while planning an activity. In fact, you can "plan" an activity within minutes. Most of the projects are made from materials you are likely to have on hand. Whenever possible they are used materials that can again be recycled when you're done. To make your teaching or caregiving life easier, a general supply list is included in the Appendix. If you have these materials and supplies organized in a cupboard, you can offer countless new activities that have real meaning for your children, at a moment's notice, with little or no preparation.

The activities are organized into three main sections and indexed for your ease. The helping hand icon shown here helps you spot the tasks that can be accomplished by parent or volunteer helpers. Delegating will allow you more direct involvement with the children.

While we've included illustrations to help clarify a few activities, I have purposely refrained from providing pictures of the projects. I want to encourage all of us to *not* teach at times, especially when it comes to process-oriented activity. When you turn to the section "In the Zoo," for example, you will find a number of possible ideas that allow the children to make animals. You no doubt have books about animals on hand. These can help the children check out what animals do look like. But don't suggest that children make theirs to look any particular way. If I had shown a model of the construction paper animals, you might unconsciously channel the children into mimicking that design. Instead of having a preconceived idea of what the children will make with the various materials, expect diversity. Encourage ingenuity and individual expression. If the child makes an animal by putting down a construction paper circle with a little bubble on top, accept her "My cat fell in the well." As that child continues to have her art work accepted, she will risk more complicated pieces. Eventually, if we don't push her, she will be drawing the cat itself. Affirm the children at their various skill levels. Nurture "thinking out of the box."

When I encourage beginning adult writers, I tell them, "The best way to improve your writing is to write." The same holds true for children's artistry. If we allow a child unending opportunities with crayons, markers, scissors, paste, and so on, we will allow him to improve his skills and enable him to listen to his inner promptings. Stay away from models as much as possible. Encourage the children's own observations and responses.

I think it's time we take advantage of the most powerful learning opportunities available, those that engage the personal lives of the children themselves. Imagine a child who's about to make a long family trip to visit a sick grandmother. Now picture the release of anxiety, and the sense of group belonging that child has (essential for a smooth reentry upon returning), as she serves up the farewell-day snack, Suitcase Sandwiches. Can you imagine your relief in being able to flip to a section of activities specific to a child's terrifying experience with fire, or family fights, or the birth of a pet? You'll find activities for responding to changes, to work that matters in a child's life, and to real family play times. Keep a list of the children you've individually acknowledged, looking for items in this guide to match special attention to each child in your care.

As your children's inner lives come out, celebrated, honored, and shared, you may find a whole new level of satisfaction in teaching. Enjoy, and let me know how the activities work for you.

Introducing Three Characters

We encourage language development in young children because interacting through language allows children to relate positively to the world around them. Even a child's tirade can be positive, because words are used instead of a physical outburst. Language also enables children to make sense of confusing feelings and events.

The characters in this book are here to give voice to parts of the inner child. Those of you who are familiar with puppets and dolls as play therapy tools know how effective a character can be in helping the inner child to speak. What's difficult to say outright, face to face, is easier for a child to say through conversation with an inanimate friend. Please note "Expand on the Topics with Flannel Board Activities" in the Appendix for ways to help children express their inner feelings in addition to interacting with these characters.

First I'd like you to meet Winger. As a little sprite with an elfish voice, Winger becomes the archetype of an imaginary friend. He speaks, often disarming truths, from the inner child. Because Winger can say what's on his mind and in his heart, he'll be a welcome friend to the classroom, however you use him.

Winger can be enlarged for bulletin boards and used as a special guest at birthdays or other gatherings. In the Appendix, you'll also find an easy-to-make puppet pattern for Winger. He can be worked into any type of "circle" time, used one-on-one between teacher and child, or be available for puppet plays. If you use Winger to help children express their feelings, be sure to have him mirror what they've already stated. Don't use Winger to direct the children into what they *should* feel.

Skippety is the fun-filled, enthusiastic, innocent child in us all. She loves language, plays with words, and talks constantly. Skippety tries out verses in a running commentary, her topics ranging from silly to serious. You can use her character to enhance activities, and you can use her as a model, for the children's own experimenting with sound and words.

Now we come to Weaver Finch who travels through stories in her mind. She also models active involvement in the world, even though she's physically confined to a wheelchair. Weaver Finch listens, and comforts, rolling children along with her into the heart of her tales. She remembers and connects people, events, and ideas in a child-friendly way.

With Weaver Finch, children can spin their own stories. Again, use the stories here as stepping-stone models for what needs to be said in your group. And remember, Weaver Finch is not a vehicle for morals instruction. She's more like a dear old friend.

I mentioned "group myth" earlier. Group myth develops when each child and family brings personalities, interests, and experience together, co-mingling in an almost surreal way. No two groups have the same myth. One group's favorite activity may be Teddy Bear space travel, while another group doesn't pay much attention to stuffed animals but is intrigued with insects or caves. The group myth transcends any curriculum or planning. Without following a time-table or a prescribed path, the myth just evolves out of the group's combined inclinations, enriching the fabric of your shared time. With my book, *Heart to Heart Caregiving,* I offered providers activities and support for this type of personalized caregiving. In *What's Up?* a whole new level of myth may evolve as Winger, Skippety, and Weaver Finch become a part of your days.

The phenomenon of group myth depends in part on the teachers' skills. If one teacher uses puppets comfortably, Winger will probably join her circle time often. Another teacher might build a home for the three characters, right in the classroom. The characters' images could be copied and pasted onto cardboard backing to be used as stand-up figures, enabling the children to invite Skippety, Winger, and Weaver Finch into their play as needed. I would love to hear how the characters have entered your group myth.

Since language is only one of the developmental areas we wish to nurture in children, communication with the characters is but a part of this holistic individualizing approach.

Now, on with the activities!

Section

1

Family Play

In this section you will find activities acknowledging family play. With so many adults nowadays trying to juggle work and home, parents need encouragement for the unencumbered play they do with their children. And children can be gentled by a memory of simpler times, when being loved didn't necessarily mean getting a bigger toy or being taken on a more extravagant vacation.

This section will affirm family activities, placing a value on having fun together without it entailing great expense. While I've included a few examples that do require money, I've focused mostly on simple, no-cost experiences. Reading a book under an apple tree or going for a walk are only old-fashioned in that they're time-honored ways of being with our children. Parents, grandparents, and other family members who take time for real interaction with their children, no matter what their economic stature, deserve our applause. Here are follow-up activities that validate family events, regardless of income. These activities may help a greater spectrum of children feel proud of their family life.

To the Beach

I understand many schools and centers aren't anywhere near a beach. The activities in this section will work for children of families who have enjoyed a beach of any kind, whether it's a seashore or a river beach. Even some city parks have "beaches" of sorts by their wading pools. I included "To the Beach" because it is a low-cost outing that many families do enjoy.

Feather Painting

Using a collection of well-washed feathers from the beach, the children water-color paint with the feathers as brushes.

When done, rinse out the feathers and dry for the next use.

Project

Sand and Pebble Pictures

Set a fairly large box lid, containing sand, pebbles, and shells from the beach, out on a table. The children take turns making pictures in the sand; setting rocks in rows or shapes; smoothing, rippling, and waving the sand.

Be sure to tell the children that the sand and rocks used in these projects will be returned to the beach when you're done. Take the children with you, if possible, when returning materials to nature.

Project

Walking

Walking along the beach
with you.
Strolling along the shore.
Walking together in whatever
weather.
One, two miles, and more.

(Walk with the children as you recite the chant.)

Beach Instruments

To make a sticklophone:

Empty an old wooden picture frame.

Have the children sort beach sticks into largest to smallest.

 Using string, jute, or whatever you have on hand, help the children tie a length of string at the ends of each stick at the top and the bottom. Suspend the sticks in a row inside the frame, in order of size, tying the other ends of the string to the bottom of the frame.

Let the children use another fairly thick, but lightweight stick to tap the sticks for sound.

To make shell-canets:

 Cut two strips of cardboard, 1″ × 2 1/2″.

The children will:

Decorate one side with colored pencils or crayons.

Tape these tightly together at one end with the colored side out.

Glue butter clam shells (or other sturdy shells) on the inside, untaped ends of these strips, so the rounded parts touch.

When dry, hold the taped end in hand and tap the shell end into the other open palm to make a clicking sound.

Beach Instruments
(continued)

To make shakers, the children will:
Fill empty baking powder cans, nearly to the top
one with dry grasses,
one with wood chips,
one with sand,
one with pebbles.
Tape on lids.
Decorate paper and tape it around the cans.
Shake as rhythm makers.

Skippety on the Seashore

Millie and Mollie went
out to the shore

Trolly la la trippy-ay.

They waded in the water
and waded some more

Trolly la la trippy-ay.

Millie and Mollie found
agates and shells

Trolly la la trippy-ay.

They laughed and they
sucked in the salty sea smells.

Trolly la la trippy-ay.

Trolly la la trippy-ay,

Trolly la

Trolly la la trippy-ay.

Winger on the Beach

I'll tell you what I'm feeling:

When I hear "going to the beach" my tummy does a flip flop. I love going to the beach! An ocean beach, a river beach, a lake beach. It doesn't matter to me. I love being by the water.

Remember what it sounds like to walk on a rocky beach? It sounds all "rockle, rockle, rockle."

Course, a sandy beach is best. Sometimes I get to go barefoot. What do you like about going to the beach?

Weaver Finch on a Trip to the Beach

Come gather round and I'll tell you a story.

One summer Nana drove a whole carload of us cousins to the ocean. Oh, did we have fun!

As soon as Nana stopped the car, we ran lickety split down to the shore. Nana took snapshots of us as we skipped and splashed and jumped the sea foam.

Then Nana brought out a blue plaid blanket that she spread on the sand. By the time we were ready to eat, the warm wind was blowing in off the water. We sat on the blanket and unpacked Nana's picnic basket. There we were, eating real "sand"wiches.

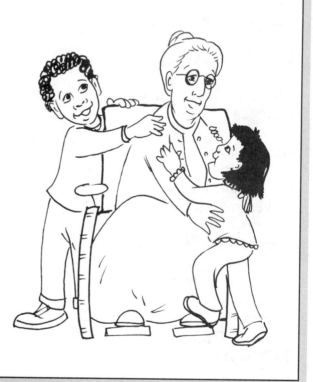

Weaver Finch on a Trip to the Beach
(continued)

After lunch Nana took us for a long walk on the beach. My friend, Sarah, found a piece of wood that was twisted in the shape of a squirrel's tail. _____ (insert a child's name from your group) found a _____ (have that child say what he found). (Continue around your group, having each child add a found object.)

After our walk, Nana needed a little rest. We younguns built a giant sand castle, with turrets and a drawbridge and moat while Nana lay watching us. Then she helped us decorate the top with wispy strands of seaweed.

Finally it was time to say goodbye to the ocean. When we got back to the car, Nana opened the trunk. We put all the treasures from our walk in an old wooden box, one with seagulls painted on the front. We let Nana take the treasures home where she kept them in a little, wild, woodsy spot in her backyard.

Years later, when we cousins went off to college and couldn't visit very often, Nana wrote me that she had taken to sitting in that woodsy back corner whenever she missed us. She'd lift out the treasures one by one, and fill herself with memories of that sparkly, wind-sandy day. She told me she wanted the cousins to take another trip together when we got to be her age, to return all the treasures back to the beach. And we did.

Finch, three, two, one. This story is done.

On a Bus Ride

Riding a Bus

Bring a large refrigerator box into your classroom.
With the children's help, draw bus windows and a door on the box.
 Cut these out.
Tape a small box to the inside front of the bus for collecting fares. Let the children bring in small chairs or cardboard boxes to sit on. A simple circle of cardboard that the driver holds in two hands will work for a steering wheel.

To enhance the play:
Add a bus stop sign or bench for those waiting a turn.

Duct tape small rings suspended by string, to the inside roof of the bus. Thread a long cord through the rings. Attach a bell on the end of the cord so children can signal their stop.

Open-faced Buswiches

For the bus, slice hoagy buns in half, lengthwise, giving each child half.
Butter.
Put a cube of cheese in the driver's spot.
Put frozen peas in rows for the passengers.
For the wheels on the bus, add slices of peeled kiwi or other round fruit, adhered with peanut butter.

Going on a Bus Ride

Children line up at a designated bus stop.

Bus driver begins alone, doing a shuffle march.

Everyone chants slowly, "Going on a bus ride, going on a bus ride . . ."

Driver stops. Rings a pretend bell.

The first child at the bus stop gets on the bus, putting hands on the waist of the driver.

Everyone chants as they go around in circle, "Going on a bus ride, etc."

Repeat, picking up more riders.

Switch drivers.

Busses

A cross-country bus goes a long ways.	*(Reach out ahead.)*
A sight-seeing bus shows the view.	*(Hand above eyes, looking side to side.)*
City busses stop and they start.	*(Make hands like wheels going around, stopping and starting.)*
My favorite? A school bus with you.	*(Point to people next to you.)*

Around Town

Set out a row of four passenger seats and a larger driver's seat. (A Captain's chair or desk chair and four child-size chairs behind.)

Have the children sit at the "bus stop," signified by a bench, a paper strip, or what-have-you.

Pass out numbered cards (1 through 4) to the first children in line.

Each time you stop for a rider, swing wide your right arm, as if opening the door. Say:

"Fifty cents	
fare, my dear.	
Watch your step	
and move to the rear.	*(Close the door.)*
Up, down,	*(Make shoulders go up and down.)*
around the town.	
Up, down,	*(Make shoulders go up and down.)*
around the town.	*(Stop bus. Open wide the door.)*
Repeat from "fifty cents."	

The person with card #1 gets on first, moves back one seat.

Each time someone gets on, everyone moves back one seat.

When the person with card #1 gets to the last seat, the next time she moves, it's out the back door. That person then hands the numbered card to the first person at the bus stop, and goes to the back of the bus stop line.

Play continues, at least until everyone has been "around town."

Skippety on Bus Rides

When I get on
a bus, I see
a whole bunch of faces
staring at me.

A whole bunch of people
short and tall.
A bus load of people
large and small.

When I get on
a bus, I hear
people talking
everywhere.

People chattering
loud and fast.
People pointing
at things we pass.

I want to find
a place to sit down,
but people are carrying stuff
from all over town.

There're people with boxes
and sacks and papers.
People with babies
and bags with diapers.

I'd like to go on
a bus ride with you.
We could carry bags
from a shopping trip too.

We'd ride up the hills
and we'd ride down.
We'd ride the bus
all around town.

Weaver Finch on Bus Rides

Come gather round and I'll tell you a story.

Once upon a time a boy and his older brother got on the city bus to go downtown. The boy stood about as tall as the back of my wheelchair and his brother was nearly tall as an adult.

On the way downtown, the bus stopped, and an old woman got on the bus. She wasn't very big herself. The woman was going to the market to buy fresh vegetables.

Now it's your turn to help me tell the story:

On the way to the market, the bus stopped. _____ got on the bus. (He/She)_____ was going to _____ to _____. On the way to _____ (the last place mentioned), a _____ got on the bus. (He/she) was going to _____ to _____, etc. (Let the children say who they would have get on the bus and where they're going, all the way around the group.)

(Older children may help you reverse the order, having each child contribute.) The bus stopped, the _____ (the last person who got on) got off. The bus stopped, the _____ got off. (The children keep telling who they had get on, until all the passengers are off the bus, except for the boy and his brother.)

The boy and his brother got off downtown. By then, they had almost forgotten where they were going, and why. Now what do you suppose that boy and his brother were up to? _____ (Get responses from as many of the children as have answers.) Could be!

Finch, three, two, one. This story is done.

Into a Butterfly Garden

Butterflies

As with all projects, this suggestion has worked for children in my care. Vary the project and materials if the children have their own ideas for making butterflies.

Here's one idea: Fold a paper. Cut out a sample butterfly wing, with the fold along the body. Open, to show two wings joined in the center. Encourage the children to draw their own wings, which they cut out.

Fold colored paper. Place the paper inside a butterfly wing pattern, matching the folds. Have the children trace a wing, then cut out a colored butterfly, twice. Finally, cut about 1/2″ in from the edge on both wing sets.

Pass out pieces of waxed paper to fit within the wings. The children can color these with crayons as intricately or simply as they wish, in patterns or solid colors.

continued

Butterflies
(continued)

Put one colored butterfly outline on top of the other. Help the children slip the colored waxed paper inside the two butterflies. Glue or staple.

Let the children tape or glue the simplest form of a body onto the butterfly. Bodies can be one-dimensional, out of paper, or two-dimensional, out of yarn wrapped around a piece of cardboard.

Hang up the butterflies so light shines through the wings.

Variation: Children can glue little pieces of colored tissue onto the waxed paper.

Butterfly Garden

Make tissue paper flowers by pulling centers of square sheets of tissue together, and winding pipe cleaners around to hold each blossom in place. Let a long end of the pipe cleaner stick down for a stem.

Let the children draw and cut out many little butterflies.

Either have them color the butterflies with colored pencils or markers, or let them squeeze a drop of food coloring onto the wings. When dry, thread a pipe cleaner through each butterfly's body, in and out. Bend the top of the pipe cleaner over at the top of the butterfly, and stick the straight end of the pipe cleaner into the flower blossom.

Children can transform a shelf or window ledge with the butterfly garden.

Butterfly Cookies

Heart-shaped cookie cutters can be used to make wings of a butterfly. Let the children use their imaginations to decorate.

Possible makings:

Cut hearts out of bread.

Butter, so that decorations adhere. (Try a healthy, soy or other vegetable, butter-like spread.)

Use a strip of cheese for the body

Cut kiwi, strips of green pepper, bananas, cherries, or grapes to make the patterns on the wings.

Add sprouts for antennas, if desired.

Skippety on Butterflies

Butterfly,

Butterfly.

How you do flit
and flutter near.

Whispering
butterfly.

Winging close, yet
I hardly hear.

Winger on Butterflies

I love it when butterflies come around. I try to follow. But I don't catch them. You know how fragile their wings are!

Butterflies trust me. When I was little, a baby butterfly landed right on my nose. Do butterflies trust you?

What do you think butterflies think?

I'll bet there's not an unhappy butterfly in the whole world.

Weaver Finch on Butterfly Land

Come gather round and I'll tell you a story.

Once there was a bright-hearted land where children planted daffodils along all the roadsides. They planted nasturtiums by the learning centers, and fuchsias in between all the businesses. And of course, they grew sweet peas and petunias in all the yards. There were flowers everywhere!

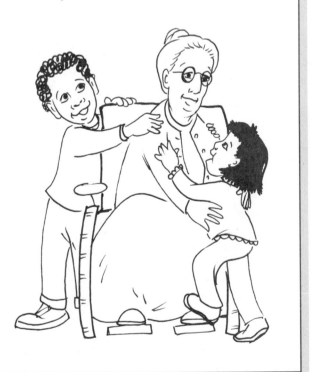

You know, now that I think of it, the children looked very much like you. There was a girl named ____. She loved to plant ____ (that child will fill in the kind or color of flower). There was a boy named ____. He loved to plant ____. (Include all the children in your group, each naming or describing a flower.)

Weaver Finch on Butterfly Land
(continued)

In late spring, with flowers well in bloom, the children would skip to the southern edge of town. There they'd sit looking. Day after day they gazed out over the hop-happy hills, until one day a child would point to something away off in the sky. The children would all shriek, "A butterfly!"

Yes, every year the butterflies returned. Great yellow butterflies with flowing wings, and tiny purple butterflies with black dots, and _____ (etc., around the room). The children danced alongside the butterflies back into town.

Every year the children would count on the butterflies. And since the children never forgot to plant flowers, year after year the butterflies counted on the children too, for their nectar-filled summer home.

Finch, three, two, one. This story is done.

On a Camping Trip

Hiking Pack

Make a back pack:

Open a large paper bag, setting it with the open end up.

Open another large paper bag. Fit the second bag upside-down inside the first.

Cut a flap in the top (which would be the actual bottom of the second bag).

Attach shoulder straps, out of two thicknesses of bag. Use heavy tape to attach the straps to the pack.

The pack works well for imaginative play hikes, or for gathering real pine cones in the park.

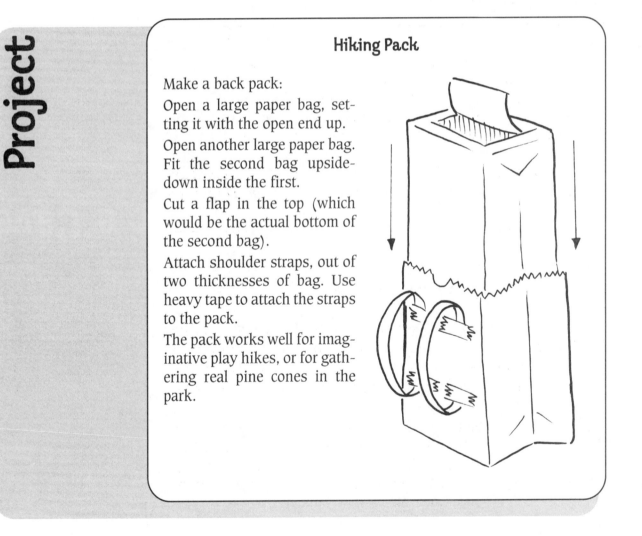

Camping

Put a tent blanket over chairs or over a rope tied between trees.
Other props:

campfire ring, made of wads of newspaper for rocks,

logs for the fire, made of rolled up newspaper, if you don't have wood handy

roasting "sticks" out of tightly rolled paper bags, taped (For safety's sake, don't use real sticks or anything pointy.)

dishpan and play dishes

dish rag and towels

fishing pole, if the children are fish-eaters

pretend tackle box (a shoe box will do nicely)

bird book and several binoculars (2 toilet paper tubes, taped together)

backpacks (see p. 27)

sketchpad and markers or pencil

Caution:

Explain that this is *pretend* camping. Children would have to be camping with the adults in their family, and adults would always be in charge of campfires. Stress once again that (a) fires are extremely dangerous, (b) no child should *ever* play with matches. Remind them, if they see a child with matches, to tell an adult.

If you're not certain that your children will leave matches and fires to the adults in their family, skip this section. Thank you.

Create a Campground

Have the snack helper fill separate bowls with celery sticks, carrot sticks, raisins, and slices of bread cut in half. The helper can also set the table with empty plates and child-appropriate knives.

Fill enough little cups of peanut butter, one for each in your group.

Children choose snack items as the bowls are passed around the table. Each child creates a campground on their own plate, cutting and spreading to make a sleeping place, a fire pit, a sitting place, or whatever they envision. Children eat their own campground.

Skippety on Camping

Here we go!
Let's spend the night!
Six brave campers
in the moonlight.

Fire's a crackling
in the pit.
On stumps and stones
we can sit.

Let's roast our supper
till it's hot;
drink cups of cocoa
from the camp pot.

Six tired campers
full of delight,
roll out our sleeping bags
in the night light.

Six big-eyed campers
hear a "Who Whooo!"
Then a great "Grruump!"
What'll we do?

Quick! Drag our sleeping bags
into the tent.
Six scared campers,
Going, gone, went.

Miniature Campground

Tent:
Roll up four sheets of newspaper, lengthwise, in one roll.
Bend the roll into a circle. Tape the ends together, fitting one end inside the other.
Reshape the circle into a triangle.
Repeat these three steps so you can have two triangles.

Miniature Campground
(continued)

Fold a large piece of tag board or construction paper in two, lengthwise.

Place the paper or cardboard over the triangles to form a tent. Tape from the underside.

Campground:

Talk with the children about what a campground looks like.

Take them on a "gathering walk," to collect dead twigs, rocks, pieces of wood, etc. with which to make a miniature campground.

Provide a boundary such as the water table or a 3′ × 3′ box, cut down to 2″ tall.

As they talk about any favorite family camping trips of their own, the children may want to add a pond or pathways using construction paper. In groups of two or three, they can take turns playing in the campground, using small cars, a van, figures, and animals.

Winger on Camping

Oh, I love to go camping! Ooooo, but it's kind of spooky at night. I don't like to walk on the path to the bathroom. Even if I do have a flashlight. And somebody to go with me.

Once I thought I heard footsteps. And bears breathing outside our tent. But Mom checked. It turned out there weren't any bears.

I'm never alone when I'm camping. That's one rule I like.

I love the smoky smell of the campground. And the chipmunks chasing up and down the trees. And roasting marshmallows. And washing our dishes outdoors. I don't like the jays so much, cuz they get after any food we leave out. But I do like the piney smell and the way the needles slip under my feet when I walk.

That's all I have to say about camping. What about you?

On a Car Trip

Skippety on Car Trips

Most of us don't like
long trips in the car.
Most of us wonder
Are we there yet? How far?

On the ride we get wiggly
and squiggly and such.
Car trips don't include
stopping that much.

We feel hungry and thirsty
and need to get out.
The driver keeps driving
till we all want to shout.

Finally we get there.
Grab the bat, ball, and snack!
Hurry! Have some fun
before we have to drive back!

Car Trip

Collect objects such as these to enable the children to reenact a particularly memorable car trip.

a small suitcase

day pack

towel, wash cloth

extra shirts

oversized pretend cardboard toothbrush (so the children don't actually put it in their mouths)

books

drawing paper and pens

Set up chairs in lines, as the seats of a car or a van.

Cars for Imaginative Play

The children can make cars out of small boxes, such as a rectangular tissue box or a small shoe box. Here are some ideas:

Glue on construction paper windshields and doors. Either draw on the wheels or cut out cardboard wheels and glue them on.

Use very small boxes for suitcases. Thin strips of cardboard can serve as "luggage racks."

Pack little bitty sack lunches.

Use "round people" or doll house figures as families, to play going on a car trip. Some children will make their own people.

Experiment with taking the cars to the block corner to make roads, bridges, or mountain passes, according to their design.

Snack

Suitcase Sandwiches

The children will fill warmed pita bread with their choice of the following:

sliced chicken (roll up for a towel)

celery sticks (for toothbrush)

cheese slices (for pants and shirt)

a cereal piece, such as any Chex cereal (for a book to read)

a grape (for a stuffed animal)

The children arrange the items in their "suitcase," before eating.

Winger on a Car Trip

One time we went for a drive on this winding road. I was reading a book in the back seat. Real soon my eyes felt hot. And my stomach started getting all smooshy inside. My mouth got water in it, even though I didn't drink anything. And then, SPLAT! I threw up. Right on my book. I didn't even know the throw up was coming.

We had to stop for me to get cleaned up. That ride wasn't fun! We've had good car rides though. Sometimes my mom starts singing. Then another of us will sing with her, then another and another, until everybody in the car is singing away.

I know a family that sings when they take car trips. They all sing at the same time. Only in their family, each person in the car sings a different song!

Weaver Finch on a Car Trip

Come gather round and I'll tell you a story.

Once I took a group of children on a car trip. I had a fancy car at the time, a sleek car that we called Sunsong. Now that was something of a magic car. On the outside it looked mighty near normal, long and low, but normal enough. But on the inside! Oh, my my. When I would open the right rear door, and the children would start piling in, why that car of mine would expand inside. It seems I always had just the right amount of seats and seat belts.

We were used to riding together. On this car trip we were going to visit a girl who had moved out to the country. She wasn't able to live in the city anymore because of something to do with her breathing. We all wanted to see Clarissa and her new farm. There was _____, and _____ (list all the children in your group, one by one).

"Seat belts everyone?" I called out from the driver's seat.

"Yep." "Unh huh." "You betcha." "Click click." "All righty!" and so on, the children called back. And off we went to Upper Hanokey Falls.

I was following the road signs, but somewhere I must've made a wrong turn. By the afternoon, I was completely lost, so I stopped at a Gull Station to get directions. While I filled up the gas tank, the children went together inside the store to ask which way we should go and what to look for on the way. I paid for the gas, and everyone climbed back into Sunsong. But before I'd even turned on the ignition, the children started talking at once.

"Seat belts everyone?" I interrupted them from the driver's seat.

"Yep." "Unh huh." "You betcha." "Click click." "All righty!" and so on, the children called back.

"Ok, everybody. Tell me one at a time, what should I look for and what do I do next?"

"Well," Barry began, "Go until you come to a big lake. Turn right."

Weaver Finch on a Car Trip
(continued)

(Invite the children to share, what you will see next . . . a red barn, a field of corn, etc. and what you should do next, such as go around a curve, go up a hill, etc.)_____ and _____, etc.

Amazingly enough, the directions worked. Soon we were pulling into the little village of Upper Hanokey Falls. And before we knew it, five miles out of town, we were turning into Clarissa's driveway. Unfortunately, we only had time for tea. And a quick tour around the farm. All too soon, because of the long drive home, we had to say goodbye. I opened the right rear door, and everybody piled into Sunsong. We all waved at Clarissa as I headed out the drive.

"Seat belts everyone?" I called out.

"Yep." "Unh huh." "You betcha." "Click click." "All righty!" and so on, the children called back.

Before we knew it, we were returning through Upper Hanokey Falls. Since it was much later than we'd planned, I stopped at a pay phone and gave everybody nickels and dimes and quarters to call their families, right there in the one and only block of downtown Hanokey. Then I treated the whole group to _____. (Ask your group what they would like for supper?) Or, I would've treated them to supper, if the town had had a restaurant. As it was, we were lucky to get a cone apiece at the local ice creamery. We ate our ice cream cones on old-fashioned picnic tables as a troop of crows danced a soft claw on the roof of my car.

"Seat belts everyone?" I called out, as they piled back into Sunsong.

"Yep." "Unh huh." "You betcha." "Click click." "All righty!" and so on, the children called back.

Some of the little ones fell asleep, but the older kids played guessing games in between helping me with directions. Soon enough we were to the freeway, where I knew my way home. By then, even the older children were getting drowsy.

Before long though I was arriving at their doorsteps, sleepy kids greeted by eager families. (If time permits, go around the group.) _____ (one child at a time) jumped out, greeted by _____ (a family member or friend) until Sunsong was empty, and I drove myself home.

Finch, three, two, one. This story is done.

Into a Cave

Caution:
Tell your students, parents, and helpers that children should never go into a cave without an adult. Caves can be dangerous. It's easy to get disoriented and lost in a cave, and caves can cave in. I include spelunking because, in some areas, cave exploration offers fascinating family fun. *If you're not certain that your children will stay out of caves, unless accompanied by an adult, skip this section. Thank you.*

Caves

Create a cave in one corner of a room. Have the children help you cover chicken wire with either tissue paper or paper maché. Let them paint their cave black.

They can add green ferns or moss around the outside, made out of construction paper or yarn.

Decorate the inside with construction paper bats. Here are possible outlines for you to duplicate, if you wish.

continued

Imaginative Play

Caves
(continued)

Let the children place their biggest teddy bear at the back of the cave.

Make mining lights using strips of black paper taped around the children's heads. On the front, have them tape on a cut-out single section from an egg carton. Glue a circle of yellow construction paper in the egg hole, for the light.

Spelunking

(Cavers, or spelunkers, explore caves.)

Have children stand in a line or semi-circle about four feet apart. The adult stands at one end holding a long thick rope. (If you don't have a rope, try this with a pretend, *invisible* rope.) Tell children, for safety, they must wait until the spelunking rope gets to them.

You will walk, in a sideways, bent-kneed fashion, as if crouched down in a cave. One by one, you will pass by the children, and they will grab on at the end of the line. Hold the rope with your right hands. With your left, pretend to hold cavers' lights at your foreheads.

Spélunking.	
Spelunking.	
We will go a hunkering	*(Move sideways, in a crouched*
into the deep dark cave.	*position.)*
	(Stand up. Pretend to bump your head on the top of the cave, crouch down again.)
Grab a'hold. Come.	*(Stop, so next child can grab onto rope.)*
Creep into the cold.	*(Continue moving sideways.)*

(Continue chanting, until all children are in.)

(Stop. Pretend with the children. What do you see? What does it feel like in the cave? Then, reversing your direction, head out of the cave.)

Spélunking.
Spelunking.
We will go a hunkering
out of the deep dark cave.
Remember to keep a'hold,
till we're out of the cold.

(Announce when you're out of the cave. Everyone lets go, so you can coil up the rope.)

Fossil Prints

Have children put about 3" of dirt in a dishpan, then smooth it flat.

Let them place leaves on the dirt, laying them out flat, without the leaves overlapping.

Very carefully, cover the leaves with a piece of plastic wrap.

Then let the children sprinkle more dirt, lightly and evenly, over the leaves, until all are covered about 2" thick.

Next place folded newspapers on top. Let children press down, with their fingers spread wide to give somewhat even pressure.

If you wish, place a couple of large blocks on the newspaper to continue pressure.

Put the date on a slip of paper, which you tape on the top. Leave for at least a month.

When you go to uncover the leaves, explain very briefly that this is something like how leaves or animal bones are uncovered underground. Let the children use spoons to carefully scoop out the dirt. Have them stop when they get to the plastic wrap. You then gently lift the plastic off the leaves. Slowly lift the skeleton of each leaf, and look at its print in the dirt.

Cave Paintings

Present this activity with something like:

A long, long time ago, people painted stories on the walls of caves. They didn't have malls, or stores, or supply cupboards, so they made their paint out of plants or crushed rocks or dirt.

We can make cave paintings. Pretend this gray paper is the cave wall. (You'll want to use a colored paper light enough for the homemade paint to show up.)

What could we make our paint out of? (dandelions, charcoal, bricks, wild berries, what-have-you)

Let the children help you gather the materials, and mash and mix the paints. If you have access to an overgrown area, the children can also help gather grasses, which you tie onto twigs, for brushes. If you live in a city, and don't have materials available, use previously collected (and washed) feathers for brushes.

Caver's Obstacle Course

Talk about how cavers crawl through small spaces.

Make an obstacle course out of chair tunnels, bean bag cushions to climb over, narrow passages made out of blocks, etc.

Let the children practice moving through the caver's obstacle course.

Caves

Melt, using a ratio of
3/4 C. peanut butter
1/4 C. chocolate chips
1/4 C. milk powder
Drizzle over two 5 oz. packages of crisp Chinese noodles.

When barely cool, pass out blobs on plates. Children can form their caves before eating.

Shadows

If possible, have the children bring flashlights to school.

Hang two sheets vertically, with a passage in between, so children can watch from either side, and the space between the sheets will be confined somewhat, as in a cave.

Be sure to leave a light on in the room. The flashlight movement will show up perfectly well in dim light.

Let children experiment with shadows on the sheets by taking turns shining their lights, from inside the two sheets. If you've just hung up one, children take turns behind the sheet, while the others sit on chairs in the viewing area.

Winger on Caves

I went with my grandma and grandpa into a big cave. I didn't want to wear my coat. It was real sunny outside. But inside the cave, it was freezing cold. Grandma was right. I was glad I had my coat after all.

I kind of liked the scary, squeezy feeling I got in my stomach. We climbed down and down these stone steps, way down into the earth.

When Grandpa turned off the lantern, just to trick us, my insides went "Eeeeps!" It was darker than darker than dark.

Here's what I'm thinking. Be sure you never go in a cave alone, even a small one. Caves can be dangerous. The top of the cave could fall in on you. Only go into caves that have been checked out by experts. Some caves have passages and rooms. We're not like bats. We're not used to bouncing our voices off the walls, and getting the sound waves back to help us know where we are in the dark. It can be easy to get lost. Only go in big caves, like the one I went in with Grandma and Grandpa. And go with a guide who knows the way out!

Going Fishing

Remember to encourage respect. Some children and families do not eat meat, so they would not go on a fishing trip. Talk about differences. Allow children to choose whether or not to participate in activities, based on their family beliefs.

Underwater Hanging

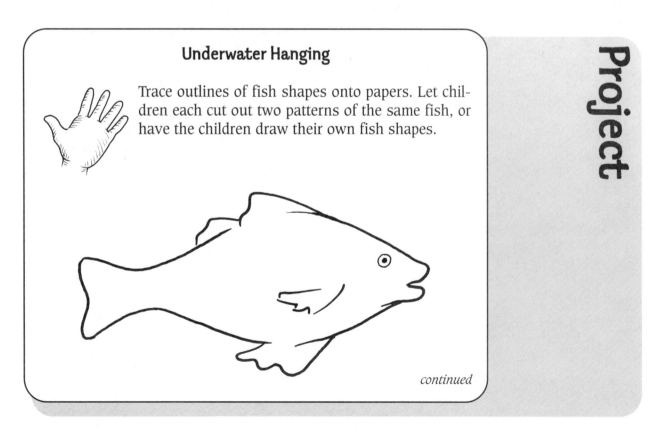

Trace outlines of fish shapes onto papers. Let children each cut out two patterns of the same fish, or have the children draw their own fish shapes.

continued

Underwater Hanging
(continued)

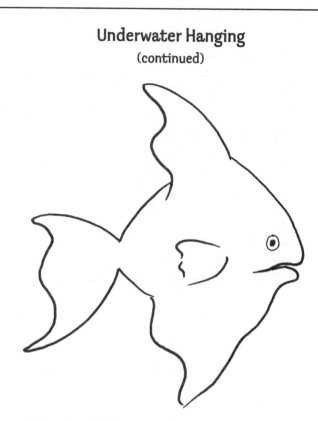

With your help, the children staple two-thirds of the way around the two matched-up fish shapes.

Then they stuff the inside of their fish with recycled tissue paper. Help them finish stapling the sides together.

Let the children paint their fish, using bright colors. They may want to take breaks to let the base color dry before painting on spots, stripes, or whatever.

Hang these fish in a corner of the room, designated as Underwater.

Let the children make vegetation by cutting long narrow strips of paper, painted green. Roll the paper tightly around a dowel. Have the children pull out the dowel. The long curls can be stapled to each other, so several curls hang off of one "stem." Hang the curls in the underwater corner.

Fishing

wrapping paper tubes for poles (If you have the time, cut the tube lengthwise. Roll the tube as tight as possible, and tape or rubber band to hold.)

string for fishing line

paper clips for hooks

shoe box for tackle box

large wooden blocks for the shore

fry pan and spatula

a cardboard box, for the camp stove

large cardboard bricks made into an indoor boat

sandbox or simple rope outline for an outdoor boat

Splatter Fish

Using fish outlines again (from "Underwater Hanging"), have children cut out one fish each.

Using round objects, from 1/2" to 1" diameter, help children trace several circles, which they then cut out.

The children can position the fish on construction paper, placing the circles to bubble out the fish's mouth. Children may put the fish and bubbles anywhere they want, of course.

Demonstrate for older children how to scrape a popsicle stick backwards across a toothbrush, to splatter over the fish and bubbles. When painted, lift off the fish and circles.

Younger children can simply glue their fish and circles onto their papers and paint with a brush or a sponge however they like.

To a Fishing Hole

Take your fishing pole
to a fishing hole.

(Hold pretend pole over shoulder.)
(Hold up, like it's resting on ground.)

continued

To a Fishing Hole
(continued)

Toss in the line   *(Cast.)*
and you'll feel fine.   *(Both thumbs up, moving back and*
                                   forth like wipers.)

Take your fishing pole   *(Repeat three lines of motions.)*
to a fishing hole.
Toss in the line
and the fish jump.   *(Abruptly, jump up.)*

Skippety on Fishing

I like going fishing
if the fishies don't get caught.
I like to see the fishies
in the lake, not the pot.

I know that people catch them
and they're very good to eat.
But watching fishies dart and glide
is my kind of treat.

Weaver Finch on Fishing

Come gather round and I'll tell you a story.

Once upon a time there was a girl and her great-grandmother. They lived on a bay by the wide open sea, a bay that also was the seasonal home to migrating Dunlins and Western Sandpipers.

During the fall, winter, and spring, when the water in the bay was choppy and cold, the girl went to school. But in the summer the water smoothed out. Then, almost every day, the grandmother took her great-granddaughter out in their double-hulled boat. Even though it was the safest boat in the bay, the girl and her great-grandmother always wore their life jackets.

The great-grandmother had to pull on the engine cord, but once started, the girl steered the boat herself, out past the docks, out past the tide bar, out of the mouth of the bay. She liked it best when Great-grandmother told her to head up around the cliffs, to their calm spot, just off the kelp bed.

It'd been several years since Great-grandmother taught her great-granddaughter how to bait a hook. The girl easily threaded chunks of herring onto both their hooks. That particular morning they were soon drifting against the pull of the anchor, with their lines stretched away from the boat. The girl sipped from her favorite mug. She always looked forward to that big cup of cocoa, which Great-grandmother gave her once their lines were in the water. They listened to the gulls overhead. The crows too were making a fuss up in the shore pines along the cliff. Sun glinted off the water. It was one of those days when the rhythm of the sea and the salt air made the great-grandmother want to fall asleep. Hmmm. . . . She did.

The girl watched the sky in case the calm weather changed. She watched and listened to the water. Before long, she felt a nibble on her line. The girl jerked up on her pole just as Great-grandmother had taught her. Then, wheeeee! The line went whizzing out of her reel. Great-grandmother woke up as the girl braced herself to begin reeling in what felt like the biggest fish she'd ever caught.

The girl bent over from the pull on the pole. Great-grandmother reminded her that no catch was worth getting yanked overboard. Bracing herself better, the girl slowly cranked the handle on her reel. Ever so carefully she pulled in the line. Finally, after

continued

Weaver Finch on Fishing
(continued)

what seemed forever, alternately cranking and letting the line rest, the girl spotted the silvery flash of the fish underwater.

Great-grandmother could tell, the girl's catch was a big one, over 20 pounds. The girl kept winding the reel, and when the fish got close enough to the surface, she turned the tip of the pole in towards the side of the boat. Great-grandmother reached out with the net and hefted the fish in at their feet.

That was quite a proud day for the girl. Not only did she manage to bring the fish ashore, but the neighbors saw her coming in with her catch. You understand, this was a fishing village, which relied on the ocean for food. All the girl's friends ran down to the shore. Her relations started up a fire in the big pit. The girl's fish, along with Great-grandmother's tomatoes, potatoes, and tiny sweet corn, fed a passel of people on the beach that night.

Finch, three, two, one. This story is done.

To a Horse Ranch

Imaginary Horse

The children can help you make pretend horses. Remember, their imaginations can make just about anything *seem* like a horse:

Crumple newspaper into a horse's body and head.

Use masking tape to hold the bundles in place.

Cover by taping on strips of butcher paper.

Poke sticks in for legs, and secure with tape.

Braid and affix yarn for a tail.

Cut lengths of yarn for the mane. Tape these on the horse's neck.

Paint eyes and mouth.

Let dry.

Horse Ranch

Use horse, just made, in an established area for outdoor play.

Or use smaller, plastic horses in a cut-down box for indoor play.

Let children make a ranch. They might:

Use dirt for a hillside, with sticks for the fences and corral.

Make a river and pond with strips of foil or construction paper.

Make a pasture with grass for grazing. Green construction paper strips, snipped along one edge, and glued, even to a piece of newspaper, can make a great pasture, unless you have grass for the real thing.

Ride the Ponies

Stand in a circle with the children.
The adult is the caller, as in a square dance.
Caller:

Ride the ponies round the ring!	*(Everyone circles round.)*

Everybody:

Canter, canter, canter.	*(Slapping legs, like riding.)*

Caller:

Cross two ponies in the center.	*(Everyone stops. Caller calls two people opposite each other in the circle. They canter across the diameter, taking each other's places. Everyone else continues making the slapping rhythm on their legs, without moving from their spots.)*

Caller repeats "Ride the ponies. . . ."
After everyone's gotten a turn to cross the ring,
Caller:

Cool your ponies to a walk.	*(Everyone walks around the circle.)*

Everyone:
Good pony-o.
Caller:

Whoa! Whoa!	*(Everyone stops.)*

Everyone:
Whoa! Whoa!

Caller:
Time to feed your horse some oats.

Everyone:

Neigh. Neigh.	*(The children let their horses eat.)*

Pretend Stable

Even an area partitioned off in the simplest of ways, by blocks or a small bureau, can be imagined a stable.

The children can gather dry grasses from round your play yard for "hay" and seed pods for "oats."

Make pretend horses out of:

rocking horse

stick horses

piano bench

a long narrow box

Gather currying tools:

a brush

a large comb

a hoof pick (any plastic curved toy piece will do for pretend)

If you haven't had experience with horses, you may want to know more about a hoof pick. To informally "demonstrate" the pick's use, simply join the play; I prefer *playing* with the children to making a *lesson* out of their imaginative time. The hoof pick is used to clean the bottom of a horse's hooves. Stand alongside one leg of a pretend horse, facing the rear. Reach down and lift up the horse's leg. Bend the leg at the joints, resting the hoof on your knee. Using the pointed end of the hoof pick, scrape the bottom of the foot. Children find imagining much easier than we do. If your horse facsimile doesn't actually have hooves, just pretend clean the part of the foot that would be a hoof.

Caution:

Never allow preschool children to be near real horses' hooves. Cleaning horses' hooves is reserved for experienced equestrians who're tall enough and strong enough to handle a horse's leg and weight. *If you care for or teach children who have access to horses, and you suspect they might try the real thing, simply skip the hoof cleaning activity. Thank you.*

Make bridle and reins out of:
bathrobe cords, small lengths of rope, or braided yarn
As with any play, be sure an adult supervises for safety.

Skippety on Riding

Giddy up horsey!
Take me away,
out past the barn,
out past the hay,
onto the trail
that leads o'er the hill.

When Cook
rings the bell,
We'll be riding still.

Imaginative Play

Horse Trainer

One person is the horse trainer. The trainer holds a short, rolled-up newspaper baton. Set agreements that this is the new, positive type of horse training, done with the mind and motions, not physical force.

The other children are horses. They may have bells tied on their shoes, if you like.

The trainer can pair up horses.

They ride around the ring.

The trainer can set out a cushion or other small, low object for the horses to jump over.

Children take turns being the trainer.

Winger on Horseback Riding

Some people think a barn smells pe-uy. I think the barn has a good smell, like my Great Uncle Chester.

I went to a barn a little while ago, one where I'd taken riding lessons. I was going to get out a horse to ride. The horse nearly stepped on my toe. Yow! That would have hurt.

I told the horse, "C'mon outside with me." But the horse wouldn't come. I was going to get on, but the horse backed up. I almost fell in the mucky stuff. Lucky for me, the groom came by and led my horse out to the gate. She boosted me up and said, "Have fun!"

My horse took off, galloping, galloping up the hill. I couldn't get it to Whoa! I couldn't get it to turn where I wanted. All I could do was hold on tight. Finally, when my horse was all worn out, it walked into the corral. I slid off the horse, and it went back to munching hay.

You know what? I was made to fly. I'm going to leave the riding to someone else.

Weaver Finch on Ponies

Come gather round and I'll tell you a story.

When I was a girl, I had a pony. Almost everybody had a pony those days. My pony's name was Bluebell. She was fit as a fiddle. Every afternoon Bluebell and I went riding.

I lived down the road from _____. (Name first child in group.) He had geese in his front yard. The geese made honking sounds whenever I came round. (Make the sounds together.) _____ (had a pony.) (Have the child say his own name.) The pony's name was _____. (That child names a pony.) _____ (the child's name) and _____ (the pony's name) and Bluebell and I went riding.

We lived down the road from _____. (Repeat all around the circle, adding children's names and their ponies as you go.)

Bluebell and _____ (Repeat all the horses names, in order.) were tired. We took them home for a rest. When I said goodbye to _____ (the first child), what do you think the geese said?

Finch three, two, one. This story is done.

At the Laundromat

Laundromat

Make a pretend laundromat with cardboard boxes:
a row of washers (even two boxes can make a row)
a row of dryers (front loading)
money slots in the machines
play money
baby clothes to pretend wash and dry
The children can play as families. You might also suggest someone being manager with pretend cleaning equipment and the repair person with tools for fixing the machines.

Imaginative Play

Washing Clothes

Set up an area for washing the home-corner doll clothes.
Depending on what's feasible for your facility, hang an indoor or outdoor line for clothes drying. Make sure to put it out of any traffic flow areas. The children can use workable clothespins. Or you might use a wooden clothes rack.
Let the children determine when the clothes are dry and ready to take down, fold, and put away.

Activity

Folding Clothes

Set up a place for hangers.

Bring in shirts with various buttons, zippers, and snaps. Children get practice fastening as they hang up the clothes.

Bring in a pile of socks.

The children can match and roll the socks into pairs.

Bring in a laundry basket full of towels, from large to hand towels to washcloths.

Folding clothes can be fun.

Laundromat Books

 Using one of your pre-made books (see Appendix), work with the child who regularly goes to the laundromat. Prepare a book for the next laundromat outing. Write in the key words or the questions below, one to a page, and have the child or a family member draw a sketch of each.

How many *washers*?

How many *dryers*?

How many *floor tiles*?

How many *tables*?

How many *chairs*?

How many *chair legs*?

How many *people* in the laundromat?

Children who can count will have fun putting the totals on each page. The number writing can be done by an older sibling or family member. Or you can show the child how to tally the counting. The acknowledgement and the process matter, not precise totals. The child can bring the book back for sharing.

On Laundromats

Swish, swish,   *(Hands to the left, then right.)*
Slugga, chugga.   *(Hands in front, one fist on top*
                                 of another, moving up and
                                 down.)

Swish, swish,   *(Repeat above.)*
Slugga, chugga,
Goes the washing machine.
Our clothes are getting clean.

Bump, bump   *(Hold hands limp in front;*
                                 swing hands in a circle in front
                                 of one's body.)

Tumble, tumble.   *(Repeat.)*
Bump, bump,
Tumble, bumble.
Watch our clothes going round.   *(Swing head in circle, too.)*
Once dry, they make no sound.   *(Stop. Hold hands out, rigid.)*

Winger on Making the Laundromat Fun

Have you ever been to the laundromat? We go every week.

Cleaning clothes at the laundromat sure takes a lot of time. We wait and wait. Sometimes we bring a game to play, or paper and crayons for drawing. Poppa reads aloud to make the time go faster. Still, getting our clothes clean can take hours. Talking with people helps. I usually see the same people every week. They're my laundromat friends.

I like when the clothes are dry. We fold them up in stacks. I always put my face in the towels. Those towels make for good nose warmers. And Poppa lets me roll up the socks.

Maybe you don't go to the laundromat all the time like we do. Maybe you just go to wash big things, like comforters or sleeping bags. Laundromats are sure good for that.

Weaver Finch on Town Laundromats

Come gather round and I'll tell you a story.

Once there was an unusual town. The people did most everything together. They cooked their meals together. They brushed their teeth together. They even washed their clothes together. Yep! Everyone in town went to the one big laundromat to get their dirty clothes clean. The laundromat owners were very important people in that town.

As the years went by, the laundromat owners took on more responsibility. It got so whenever there was something the townspeople needed to clean, and it wouldn't fit in the washers, the laundromat owners would order in a new machine to do the job.

Soon the townspeople were asking for a machine to wash their bicycles. The owners put in a bicycle wash. Then the gardeners wanted a way to wash their lawn mowers at the end of the summer. The owners adapted one of the bicycle washers for the lawn mowers.

Then the townspeople wanted a place to wash their cats and dogs. So the owners put in a dog and cat aisle. What do you suppose those machines looked like? _____ Before long they got more machines. Tell me some of the things you think the townspeople washed in the new machines: _____, _____, and _____

Finally, one Saturday there was a big commotion at the laundromat. One of the townspeople had brought in a _____. The laundromat owners had always helped out the community. What do you suppose the owners did next? _____

You know what, you're right. And the whole town got together at the laundromat to celebrate the new machine.

Finch, three, two, one. This story is done.

To the Park

Imaginative Play

Miniature Park

Designate a large table top or a cardboard box with sides cut down as "the park."

Help the children build:

a slide out of a cereal box

a merry-go-round out of an oatmeal box

swings out of another cereal box

a sand box

teeter totter out of a small box notched for the base, with a popsicle stick for the see saw

Assemble a set of small dolls, animals (dogs, cats, squirrels) for playing with in "the park." This is a great activity to honor children's capacity for using their imaginations. If you don't have a suitable set of people and animals, suggest creating them. Children can glue small scraps of construction paper on twigs to make people. For animals, wedge small sticks into a pine cone for the legs, tail, and neck. Glue on a yarn leash and construction paper head. Remember to let the children come up with their own creations. I've seen a child use a wood chip for a perfectly playable unicorn. Allowing the children to "make do" often opens the door to delight, for children and adults both.

continued

Miniature Park
(continued)

The children may play with the park one day, then decide to continue developing the play scene for several days following. Depending on the parks in their area, children may want to add:

a pond out of construction paper or foil

a fountain out of a small box, with tinfoil shreds streaming out

trees, out of cardboard, notched at the bottom with a piece of cardboard fit in sideways for a stand

bushes or flower border, with notched stands

an ice cream stand

an outdoor ice rink or wading pool, in season

Creative Movement on People in the Park

Gather the children in an area where there will be enough room for everyone to move around.

Lead the children in acting out people in the park:

a woman jogging

a man walking his dog

a girl skateboarding

a boy rollerblading

a baby in a stroller

a child feeding the ducks

Get the children's suggestions for acting out others in the park.

For flying kites and other activities with more than one step, elaborate on the movements, such as:

getting the kite out of its bag

getting it into the air

watching it soar

watching it fall to the ground

Ringbee

Children roll newspaper and tape it into a tube.

Then they bend the roll into a circle, fitting one end into the other, taping it in a ring.

Stand in a circle with the children, either outdoors or in a gym.

Toss ringbee from one child to the next, around a large circle.

If the children are old enough to multi-task, start one ringbee around the circle. When the ringbee gets half-way around, start another. Keep the two ringbees going around the circle at once.

Children can make ringbees for their families to play at the park.

Can you Roller Skate in the Park?

Have everyone stand, with you in front of the group facing them. This is like a "Sound Off" chant, where the teacher asks a question and the children answer back, motioning actions as they wish.

Leader: Can you roller skate in the park?

Children: I can roller skate in the park.

Leader: Can you hear a doggy bark?

Children: I can hear a doggy bark.

Leader: Can you jump and touch a tree?

Children: I can jump and touch a tree.

Leader: Can you stretch and bend your knee?

Children: I can stretch and bend my knee.

Leader: Can you jog around the track?

Children: I can jog around the track.

Leader: Can you picnic on a sack?

Children: I can picnic on a sack.

(Lead everyone in putting down a pretend paper sack. Sit. Pretend to eat an imaginary lunch.)

Weaver Finch on Going to the Park

Come gather round and I'll tell you a story.

Once upon a time there was a mother. She didn't have much money, but she was very rich because she had something better than money. She had three children.

Whenever she could, the mother took her children to the park. The children got to run and laugh and yell "Yippee!" (Everyone yell Yippee) _____! They got to (motion your hand going down a slide) go down a slide. They got to go around and around (motion hand going around) on a _____. (Children will provide the words while they motion with you.) They got to go back and forth (swing motion back and forth with whole arm pushing away from body) on the _____. They got to go up and down (motion flat arm, elbow to fingertips, teeter tottering) on a _____.

The mother played catch with a (motion throwing a ball) _____. Sometimes they threw the (motion throwing a frisbee) _____. And other times she pulled them around the park in their big red (motion pulling) _____.

Every so often the mother got impatient because the children didn't come when she called them (scowling, with hands on hips). And sometimes the children got a teeny bit mad at each other when one of them wouldn't share the bouncy horse (scowling again, hands on hips). But mostly they had happy times going to the park together.

Finch, three, two, one. This story is done.

To a
Pet Store

Pet Store

Make a corner of the room a pet store.

Use construction paper to draw animals or use stuffed toys for the pets.

Use boxes for the cages.

Make confetti to fill small food bags.

Add a cash register and play money.

Variation:

If your school or caregiving center has a number of pets in various classrooms, see if you can gather the cages into one room for a more realistic pet store.

These could be the store owners' pets for viewing, and the customers could "buy" the pretend ones. If customers come from other classrooms, you may want to have the children "sell" construction paper animals to avoid having to return stuffed animals later.

The Pet Store

(Stand with the children in a circle.
Move around the circle, as the song indicates, standing still only during the "What do you find in there?")

Skip to the pet store,
skip, skip, skip.
Hop to the pet store,
hop, hop, hop.
Jump to the pet store,
jump, jump, jump.
And what do we find in there?

Children are called on to fill in "what." Repeat, using the name of the animal. For example, you might start with:

Puppies in the pet store,
skip, skip, skip.
Puppies in the pet store,
hop, hop, hop.
Puppies in the pet store,
jump, jump, jump.
What else do we find in there?

Continue with whatever animals the children suggest.

Pet Food (for people)

sunflower seeds for bird seed
fish crackers for fish food
biscuits rolled in Parmesan cheese, and baked for dog biscuits
milk for cat food
pieces of red leaf lettuce or carrot for rodent food
pieces of watermelon for turtle food

Winger on Pet Stores

Oh, I do love a pet store. You know I do! My family doesn't like to take me very often. I always want to bring animals home.

Sometimes there are bunnies with floppy-down ears. Sometimes there are kittens, batting and rolling and pouncing on each other. Sometimes there are spotted fish, swim, dart, swim, dart swimming.

Once I went to a pet store and a cockatoo went whee! whee! (whistle). I thought he was whistling at me.

Once I put my hands in the mouse pen— the sign said it was okay to pet them—and six teensy mice skittered up my arms.

Once the owner let me pet a little yellow snake. The snake slithered up my sleeve. We had to take my coat off to get her out.

A pet store can be a troublesome place to visit when you love animals the way I do. I used to try to take an empty cage in the car. I thought if I had a cage along my family would let me buy a pet. Now they make me promise, "We're not getting any more pets today." If I don't promise, I don't get to go.

Of course when you need an animal, pet stores and animal shelters are great places to visit.

Weaver Finch at the Pet Store

Come gather round and I'll tell you a story.

Once there was a group of children. These were fine children! These were responsible children. These children were ready to own a pet. So they went with their teacher to Waggity's Pet Store.

When they opened the door, a rope pulled on a bell. The ringing of the bell seemed to make all the animals bark and meow and chirp and chatter all at once. When the children went into the pet store . . . oh my goodness! Right off they noticed a big, big cage that went all the way to the ceiling. The cage door stood open and outside the door a bird perched on a tall barrel. The bird had long _____ (color) feathers. Slick long _____ feathers with little tufts of _____ (another color) on their tips. You know what that bird said when they walked in the door? "Take me home!"

The children thought that was the most clever bird they had ever heard. So they asked Mr. Waggity, the owner, "How much for the bird with the long _____ feathers?"

Mr. Waggity shook his head and chuckled. "Oh, no. That bird's not for sale. That bird just wants me to take him home."

(Continue the story, giving the children the opportunity to add animals and "No" each time. Here are some examples.)
Wiggly puppy: "No, she's waitin' to get her bath and her toenails clipped."
Purry kitten: "No, that kitten's under observation because it doesn't smile. I couldn't sell someone a sad kitten, could I?"
Box turtle: "No, that turtle pulls his head in. He's much too shy."
(Let your children add animals and reasons why each one is not for sale.)

Finally, after the children had looked all around the store, the oldest child said, "You know, I don't think you want to sell any of these pets!"

"Yeah!" chimed in the youngsters.

"How come?" the older one asked.

continued

Weaver Finch at the Pet Store
(continued)

The owner hung his head. "Oh dear, right you are. You've guessed it. I can't possibly sell a single one of me pets," he crooned, scooping up a puppy. "They're might too adorable, or cuddly, or silly. Close to me, they are, in one way or 'nother." Mr. Waggity rubbed noses with the little pup. Sitting down he added, "But I am growin' weary, what with keepin' so many animals to meself."

Then Mr. Waggity thought a minute. "Say now," he began, "you look to be caring 'n kind." He sent a quizzical look to the teacher who beamed, nodding her head.

"And *responsible,*" piped up the youngest.

The teacher nodded some more.

"What do you say to comin' here in the afternoons to help with me pets? You could have all the fun that I do, and I wouldn't have to send you home with your tails a draggin.'"

Their teacher said yes. The children checked with all their families who also said yes. Mr. Waggity and the children became great friends. They loved and cared for the pets together. Sometimes Mr. Waggity asked a child to take one of the animals home for a visit. But they never sold a single pet. Not a one.

Finch, three, two, one. This story is done.

To a Pond

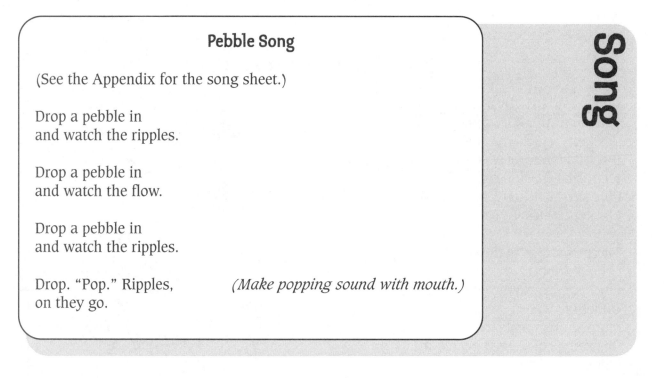

Pebble Song

(See the Appendix for the song sheet.)

Drop a pebble in
and watch the ripples.

Drop a pebble in
and watch the flow.

Drop a pebble in
and watch the ripples.

Drop. "Pop." Ripples,   *(Make popping sound with mouth.)*
on they go.

Lily Pads in a Pond

Stand with the children in a large circle. Recite the rhyme:

One, two, three and four.
Lily pads make more and more.
Call out a child's name.

While everyone recites the two-line rhyme, that child hops to the center of the circle, squats down, and holds hands out, palms up. That child then calls another child's name, and everyone recites the rhyme again while the new child hops to the center. (If the children are not yet able to hop a distance, they can walk to the center, hop once, and squat.) Each new lily pad calls in another. Repeat until everyone is in the pond.

Skippety on Driving by a Pond

When you drive by a pond
you might think it's quiet.
Chickerty, chickerty, chee.
But when you get close,
oh, the chirp, chirring, whirring!
Chickerty, chickerty, hee, tee-hee,
Chickety, chickety, chee.

There are frogs in the pond,
Grump. Ribbet.
Chickerty, chickerty, chee.
Under the water
blurp sunfish and pickerel,
Chickerty, chickerty, hee, tee-tee,
Chickety, chickety, chee.

There might be a shrew
or a vole, scurry-nibble.
Chickerty, chickerty, chee.
Clackety beetles,
water bugs, dragonflies.
Chickerty, chickerty, hee, tee-tee,
Chickety, chickety, chee.

Skippety on Driving by a Pond

(continued)

The geese and the mallard
fly in and fly out.
Chickerty chickerty, chee.
The red-winged blackbird
call kong ka-ree.
Chickerty, chickerty, chee, tee-tee,
Chickety, chickety, chee.

I thought ponds were dull.
Yes, I did. Yes, I did.
Chickerty, chickerty, chee.
Till I sat very still
and the pond came ALIVE.
Chickerty, chickerty, chee, tee-hee.
Chickety, chickety, chee!

Winger on Ponds

You know what I'm thinking? I like a pond.
I really do.
I pretend I'm a turtle lying on a log.
Or . . . I'm a frog, hopping on the lily pads.
Or maybe a beaver, gnaw, gnaw, gnawing
on an alder tree.
And how about those skit, skit scooting
water beetles?

I like the pond. It's a good place to listen. A
good place to pretend with the animals. I
like the pond. I really do. Do you?

Reading on a Blanket, under the Apple Tree

Note:
This is a perfect example of the kind of fun we can honor and encourage in all families. Reading under an apple tree doesn't cost money and is available to almost everyone. Change the type of tree, of course, to suit your locale.

Project

Book

Using your pre-made books (See Appendix), compose a story with the children, specifically for reading under the maple tree, or what-have-you.

Activity

Reading under an Apple Tree

Pack up a basket, box, or bag.
Have the children help you decide what to put in, such as:
your newly made book
a blanket
snacks
ringbees

Reading under an Apple Tree
(continued)

Even "reading under the willow tree" can become an event. As you bring eager, caring energy to the experience, the children pick up on your enthusiasm. They may take home some of this making-something-out-of-nothing (except togetherness) attitude, altering their own family's expectations of family fun.

Take your children outdoors, to read their special books under a favorite tree.

Trees in Bloom

Cut out stencils of apple blossoms and leaves.

Let the children use strips of brown paper for the trunks.

Using the stencils, they can add blossoms and leaves, or apples and leaves. Offer color crayons or markers for filling in their stenciled pictures. The children can dip Q-tips into a saucer of yellow paint to blot on the pollen centers.

More Reading

Put up a chart on the wall at the children's eye level.

Have the days for one week along the top.

In a column under the days, draw in a different-colored book under each day.

For example, draw a red book for Monday, blue for Tuesday, etc.

On Monday, the children pick books with red on the covers, to take outdoors, for a read-together-under-the-apple-tree time.

Establish a routine where the children take time to look through their chosen books, then you read one or two to the whole group.

Bringing the "Tree" Indoors

When winter weather closes in, make an "outdoor reading" area in a corner of your room.

A tree can be fashioned by twisting newspaper and paper bags in a long roll. The "tree" can be painted and stapled to a bulletin board to hold it up. Real dead tree sticks can be poked in for branches, or more rolled limbs can be taped on. Pink tissue blossoms can be tied onto the sticks.

This reading spot will appeal when the dark winter days drag on your spirit. Of course if you make the tree in late winter, your room will be ready for spring!

Gather your picnic blanket and books and enjoy the outdoors, in.

Story Telling

Make up the story of Bibbeldy Bear.

Use the paper bag back packs, from the camping section, to act it out.

Perform, informally, with the audience sitting on the blanket . . . (Yep, you guessed it) . . . under the apple tree.

Skippety on Reading under a Tree

I took my brother
by the hand.
We wanted to travel
to a far-off land.

But Mama said, "Honeys,
come with me,
We'll travel the world
from our apple tree."

Spread the blanket,
bring the snack.
Mama's going to read
Bibbeldy Bear's Pack.

Winger on Reading under a Tree

Here's what I think: We don't have to have
the most popular toys, the newest games, or
even much money to have fun together as a
family.

Our family might have one adult and one
child, or it might have a lot of people. We
can have tons of fun, no matter what our
family is like, and no matter how much
money we have.

It doesn't cost anything to read aloud.
Why, the author of this book spent hours
and hours reading aloud to her children,
and they remember those as some of their
happiest times. Whether your family has a
lot of money or not, whether your family is
large or small, whether you live in the city
or country, see if you can get reading
under a tree started at your house or in your neighborhood park. Then tell a friend or
two. Maybe they can start reading under a tree with their families also.

Weaver Finch on Family Fun

Come gather round and I'll tell you a story.

When I was a girl, our family had very little money. All the electronic games that people play now weren't even invented when I was growing up. We didn't even have a TV. I don't think I would have wanted those expensive gadgets though. We did just fine making our own entertainment.

I'll tell you why we didn't need a TV. In those days people would tell stories, or read whole chapter books aloud. We could see the pictures inside our minds.

When Saturday afternoon came round, well that was the happiest time of the week. After all the chores were done . . . and there were a lot of chores in those days, believe you me . . . we'd gather up the picnic quilt, the worn red pillow with gold trim and the lumpy blue plaid one (those were the pillows allowed outside), and a copy of whatever book we were reading. We'd take our things out under the apple tree. Mother or Aunt May would read to us until dinner time.

I liked it best when Mother had us pack out our drawing tablets and the tin box of colored pencils. Then we'd draw while they took turns reading. But when the wind would swirl sweet apple smells and the butterflies dart right past my nose, I'd sometimes have to ask Mother to go back a page. I'd find I'd drawn a butterfly atop an apple blossom, but I couldn't for the life of me remember what was happening in the story. Mother and Auntie May were used to my daydreams.

Do you have a memory of reading outdoors with someone in your family? _____ If you don't, maybe you can make yourself a memory this Saturday afternoon. Reading under a tree is great fun. Try it, why don't you.

Finch, three, two, one. This story is done.

To the Woods

Woods

Woods, woods,
woods, woods.
Listen to the birds
and hear the chipmunks.

Woods, woods,
woods, woods.
Smell the ferns
and touch the tree trunks.

Woods, woods,
woods, woods.
Perch so very still
on beds of moss green.

Woods, woods,
woods, woods.
Just like animals
who are rarely seen.

(Every time the "woods, woods" lines are repeated, raise hands in air and sway like the trees.)

The Gatherers

 Ahead of time you'll need to cut green nuts and brown nuts out of construction paper. How many children in your group? Divide that number in half, and multiply by several. That's how many nuts you'll need.

One-half of the children are trees in the forest. The trees plant themselves around the room or playground.

The other half of the children are gatherers. The gatherers carry paper baskets, some brown and some green. (You can mark baskets with green and brown bows, out of yarn or ribbon, or make green and brown baskets out of paper.)

The leader passes out several green nuts and brown nuts to the trees, giving some all green, some all brown, and some both.

On their own, the gatherers go to a tree of their choice, moving from one tree to another, gathering the same color nuts as their basket.

Only one gatherer may be at a tree at one time.

The gatherer asks, "Do you have a green (or brown) nut?" (The color requested matches the child's basket.)

If the tree does, the tree says, "Yes, I have a brown nut" (or green), and gives one of that color to the gatherer. If the tree doesn't have the color nut requested, the tree says, "No. So sorry. Go on about your gathering."

When all the nuts are gathered off a tree, the tree starts swaying in the breeze. When all the trees are swaying, the gatherers pretend to eat their nuts, then turn in the baskets to the teacher or caregiver.

The trees and gatherers switch places and the teacher or caregiver begins the game again.

Sounds of the Woods

Cut a strip of thin heavy paper, just narrower than the inside of a paper towel tube, and about 2 1/2 times as long.

Demonstrate how to fold the strip, back and forth, in one inch lengths, until the whole strip is folded.

Slide the strip into the tube so that it extends, still folded, from one end to the other. Tape the ends to the inside, 1/4″ from the end of the tube.

Sounds of the Woods
(continued)

Have the children tape paper over one end of the tube. Turn the tube so the taped-over end is down.

Have the children sprinkle 1/4 cup seeds or bits of dried twigs into the tube.

Seal the top end with a taped-on round of cardboard.

Finally, the children can color the outside with a forest motif.

When the tube is slowly turned, with one end up, then the other, the seeds make a rustling, woodsy sound.

Dirt Collages

Gather fallen leaves, seed pods, twigs, and cones, preferably on an outing when you can discuss taking fallen items from the wild only in places where there is an abundance of material. Be sure to leave plenty for nourishment of the forest floor itself. You can also return the materials when you're done.

Set your items beside a tray of rich dirt. One or two children at a time can make a collage by arranging items in the dirt. You might want to photograph the collages, if your resources allow, before removing each group's work to make way for the next.

Rubbings

materials: gathered leaves or cedar shavings

Have the children place one or two sprigs or individual leaves on a tray. Each child sets a piece of construction paper on top of the items and lightly rubs a peeled crayon back and forth over the paper. The items will show up darker than the surrounding areas.

The children can use a light green or brown water color wash over the rubbing. It will appear as if the leaves or sprigs are embedded in dirt or floating in a pool.

Winger on Walking in the Woods

Do you have someone older to take you walking in the woods? I do. And I love it.

I can smell the woods, just thinking about it. The greenness has a smell. Like moss and ferns, and nettles in the spring. I like the tingly smelling cedar boughs. The brownness under the trees has a different good smell. Fallen needles, nuts, and twigs.

Sometimes I see little fairies under the trees. And elves behind bushes, I think. There are so many hidey places. The woods must be perfect for elves. I can imagine them using acorns to drink out of. Maybe they drink rain water. And some of the big flat leaves look like elfy beds. That's what I imagine in my mind anyway. Can you picture elves swinging their legs as they sit on rocks set out in a circle, way deep in the forest? Maybe they're laughing, singing songs their grandparents taught them.

My mom and I like to sit on a log in the woods. We sit really still. And sit and sit until the birds and the deer and the fox hardly notice we're there. We don't move. Can you do that? Not move at all? Being still works really well for spotting animals. They come out of their hidey places. Mostly I see squirrels and chipmunks. They know I won't hurt them. One time a chipmunk sat right by my knee. He was chipping and chattering and nibbling on a seed. Have you ever had an animal come really close when you were in the woods?

Weaver Finch on Woods

Come gather round and I'll tell you a story.

Once there was an elf named Fern. She lived in a cottage carved out of a hollow tree, deep deep in the woods. Fern had a friend, elf himself, who lived in a tree house up the creek from her place, and away over the other side of the spruce grove. His name was Forrest.

Every morning early, after a full moon, Fern and Forrest would walk to meet each other. They'd have to go through the thick conifers, then follow the creek from opposite directions

Weaver Finch on Woods
(continued)

until they got to Meeting Falls. The big flat rock to the south of the falls marked halfway between their two homes. What a great meeting spot. Halfway, and warmed by the noonday sun. Even in winter.

Every month they would picnic together on the flat rock. Fern would bring bingle berries and licorice root. Forrest would bring whazzle nuts and peapot seeds. Besides which, they picked the prickly peach that grew on the edge of the falls.

One day about midway through their lunch, Fern and Forrest heard a rustling behind them. Forrest jumped and without thinking, covered his head. Fern quickly turned hers to see what had made the sound. Oh, it was only a whizzle-woot on her way back to her cave. Fern knew whizzle-woots were friendly, especially if you toss them a few whazzles, which Forrest did, straightaway. The whizzle-woot paused in the path, just long enough to munch down the nuts.

Pretty soon Fern and Forrest heard another sound, a scritchy scratching sound. This time Fern jumped. There, below Fern's side of the rock was a _____. Now _____ are friendly, especially if you _____. So Forrest and Fern _____, until the _____ went on its way.

When they were done eating, Fern and Forrest waded in the pool below the falls. A _____ in the pool swam right up next to them. Both Fern and Forrest jumped, and fell, splash, into the pool. But the _____ is friendly, especially if you _____. So Fern and Forrest _____ until the _____ went on its way.

By then it was time to go. The two friends said goodbye and walked separate directions back to their elf homes at either end of the deep deep woods, until the morning after the next full moon, when they would visit each other again, at the big flat rock just to the south of Meeting Falls.

Finch, three, two, one. This story is done.

In the Yard
(to Watch
a Worm)

Activity

Worm Watch

Place a layer of rocks in the bottom of a plastic tank. The children can help you fill it two-thirds full with dirt.

Let them add, especially along the sides, a rotting piece of log, dry leaves, and earthworms.

Cover the outside of the tank with dark paper or cardboard.

Keep the dirt just barely damp.

Take off the paper covers when you want to watch the worms.

Gently return the worms outdoors when you're done.

Snack

Worms in the Dirt

chocolate pudding for dirt
chopped peanuts for gravel
crispy Chinese noodles for worms

Serve in bowls. Eat with celery sticks or spoons.

Skippety on Worms

Why do we think
worms are so neat?
I'll tell you why.
They have no feet.

They have no legs
or arms or hair.
They don't have to find
something to wear.

All day and night
worms lie around.
Nobody tells them,
"Get up off the ground."

But I've been wondering
when worms wiggle . . .
Are they like us?
Do they giggle?

Worm Squeegee

Whenever you can, with the children, stop to watch worms moving across wet pavement.

When you return indoors, try various wiggles and worm movements yourselves.

Put on any instrumental music. If you have music in your collection with a one/two beat, use that. Let the children alternate between dancing as a worm, and on your call, as a person. Then switch back to being a worm.

Finally, invite the children to do the worm squeegee. If it's beyond you to demonstrate, have your most prodigious mover show the group. (Simply imitate a worm.)

Creative Movement

Worm Tracks

Use heavy white paper.

Have the children paint a thick coating of brown paint.

Using a clothespin to hold the yarn, let the children trail a 6″ to 10″ length of rug yarn through the paint. Also try several strands of yarn, braided together.

Variation:

Use slick white paper, wetted a little with water.

Let the children sprinkle on a spoonful of powdered paint.

Again, holding the yarn with a clothespin, the children can trail their worms through the alternately wet and dry terrain.

Winger on Worms

I've always liked worms. Did you know that?

Sometimes I take my shovel and dig in the compost pile. Or I lift up some leaves in the yard, and what do you know? There's a worm!

The easiest way to find a worm is to wait until it rains. Then those babies are out crawling all over the place. It's fun to take an umbrella outside. I squat down under the umbrella and watch the worms move.

I always stop to rescue worms when they need it. You know what I mean. When the pavement's drying and a worm is stuck halfway across the sidewalk, I lift it up and take it to a wormy spot. Do you do that? Sometimes my mom is in a hurry, but she's started helping me pick up the worms, so she doesn't have to wait so long.

Stop when you see a worm on the sidewalk. Or on the playground. Pick it up ever so gently and set it in the grass. Or maybe put it in a flower bed. If you do, tell the worm "Hi" for me. And listen when you rescue a worm. I always hear the worm whisper, in a little wormy voice, "Thank you."

Weaver Finch on Playing in the Yard

Come gather round and I'll tell you a story.

Once there was a family. They liked to lie in the yard. (Have the children spread out in your rug area. They can act this out while you read.)

The children were lying on their stomachs, looking for a four-leaf clover, when a worm crawled by.

The children followed the worm, inching, inching along.

The worm curled up . . . and the children curled up.

The worm s-l-o-w-l-y stretched out straight again. The children s-l-o-w-l-y stretched out straight too.

The worm twisted and twisted, and rolled itself over. The children twisted their bodies, and rolled over once too.

The worm was tired. It curled up again and fell asleep. The children weren't tired. They got up and went (to snacks, to their next activity, or what-have-you) _____.

Finch, three, two, one. This story is done.

To the Zoo

Zoo Animals

The children create their own zoo animals using:

oatmeal containers

paper towel or toilet paper tubes

cardboard triangles, folded

They will glue the pieces together, getting your help with notching, if needed. Don't be concerned about the realistic nature of the animals. Let the children create imaginary animals, which they name, if that better suits your group.

After the glue dries, the children can paint the body and faces.

They can add yarn or paper curls, as desired.

Miniature Zoo

Let the children make animals out of playdough and toothpicks.

Plastic mesh berry baskets make old-fashioned cages. (Use two, with the ends taped together if the animals are too big to fit under one.)

Talk about habitats. Let the children create a more humane zoo, with habitat areas instead of cages.

A zooscape can be made out of real rocks and sand. Make trees out of sticks with green tissue boughs.

The children will enjoy moving the animals from their cages into the habitat areas.

Habitats

First set up a playpen.

Let the children bring stuffed jungle animals to school, but confine them to the playpen.

Then allot a corner of the room for becoming a jungle habitat.

Help children hang vines of braided yarn. Let them make:

a tree out of cardboard tubing

a pool of butcher paper, painted

bushes out of small boxes, covered with crumpled paper and painted

plastic fruit hanging from the bushes or tree

Have a habitat opening day when the zookeepers move their animals from the old cage to their new habitat.

Zoo Mural

Roll a long piece of butcher paper onto the floor.

 Let the children choose from construction paper shapes in an array of colors.

The children can glue the shapes onto the paper to make their own animals. They can use construction paper for the arms, legs, and tails, or they can draw these on with markers, using the paper for the face features.

Remember to accept whatever the child envisions. Let the children create, however they imagine their animals. A square with a tail sticking out is perfectly acceptable; the child may explain that his lion is under the box.

Label below the animals with the child's name and each kind of animal, whether realistic or pretend.

Hang the mural at the children's height, when done.

Zoo Animals

Pass around food items. Let children pick what they need to make one animal of their own creation. Eat. Then pass ingredients again.

Ritz crackers
peanut butter
pretzels
grapes
raisins
apple slices
cheese chunks

Skippety on Zoo Animals

Have you ever been
to the zoo?
Have you ever seen
the white-tailed gnu?

Or watched the lemur
with striped tail?
Or Bengal tiger
or Beluga whale?

I've seen gorillas
eat piles of fruit.
Heard night-house owls
go hooty hoot.

I've seen antelopes,
and sleek gazelles,
lions in the sun,
tortoise in shells.

Have you seen a hippo,
dolphin, or crane?
The zoo's fun to visit
again and again.

Section

Family Work

A child's identity grows in part out of the work orientation of the significant adults in that child's life. "My big brother roofs houses." "My mom is a firefighter." "My dad teaches school." This section allows children to bring some of their at-home knowledge into the classroom. The activities also provide the parents with recognition for their work.

Included is a sampling of curriculum responses to a variety of jobs, suitable to any neighborhood. If you don't find a child's particular work interest, you may be able to adapt activities from a job that is somewhat similar.

Artist

Project

Sock Puppets

Make dye out of natural ingredients using items children would choose, such as:

dirt and water

dandelion paste and water

berries

Dip old white socks into one of the dyes. Hang, to dry.

Lightly stuff the toe of the sock.

Slip the sock over a toilet paper tube.

Thread large needles with embroidery thread.

Older children can sew on buttons for eyes; volunteers can help younger children.

With markers, children can draw on mouths, noses, and eyebrows as they wish.

Show how to twist a pipe cleaner around for arms.

They can glue on bits of yarn for hair.

Puppets can be used with tube still in them.

Artist's Studio

Set up an artist's studio, distinct from your "art" table. Designate a small table, preferably out of the flow of traffic, for one or two children to use at a time. Have materials set out: glue, scissors, paint, paper scraps, yarn, etc.

Projects should be child-directed. Each child can create from an array of materials, or use just one medium if desired. Again, demonstrate valuing the process. The final product's importance will be determined by each artist.

Finger Pudding

Using clean hands and clean plastic dinner plates, let children finger paint with chocolate, lemon, or vanilla pudding.

As with painting, the experience should be savored. First dish out one flavor; after the children have "painted" awhile, add a second flavor to their plates.

This is one painting you expect the children to eat.

Getting the Feel of Color

Each day for a week, set out one magazine picture on a certain table. The first day it might be a bird, the next a frog, etc.

Let the picture determine the color spectrum in the materials you set out. Each day they will be different:

a tree frog—green denim and cotton, construction paper, tissue, paints in several shades, grass (actual or imitation), etc.

a red rose—red taffeta, brocade, velvet, cellophane, yarn, tinted styrofoam and so on, according to your pictures and materials on hand.

Skippety on Making Things

Oh, Skippety,

Oh, that's me!

I'll paint the sun.

I'll draw a tree.

I'll make a
funny face in clay.

I'll braid my beads
in yarn today.

I like to make things.

Yes I do.

Come, work with me.

You can too.

Project

Group Sculpture

Cut down the sides of a large box, to make a tray. Set this tray in the middle of a table, where it won't have to be moved for a week. Have glue pots and brushes around the sides of the tray. Establish an agreement that this will be a group project. No one may remove another person's contributions, but as the work progresses, one day's work will be covered by the next.

Children can bring recyclables or safe "junk" from home. Over the course of the week, children who want to, can add to the group sculpture. Encourage talking. Model put-ups of the children's work. Show personal delight, as in "Oh, look how this twig sticks out sideways!"

Variations:

Restrict the materials to egg cartons, or to toilet paper and paper towel tubes.

Make several trays and limit the sculpting to pairs.

Winger on Artists

Here's what I think about being an artist: Being an artist is like having a bird song fly right out of your heart. And the best thing: anybody can be an artist!

Look around at the different colors we like! (Point to children, naming the specific colors on their clothes, or their drawings.) And shapes! (Hop up. With Winger show the children specific shapes and their uses.) Circles make balls and clocks; squares make blocks and windows; so do rectangles. (Find shapes around your room, in an excited, rather than instructive way.) There are so many shapes to use in our drawings and sculptures.

And what about our favorite things? Smooth rocks, and slippery cloth, sparkly sequins, stars, and hearts. We can find artists' materials all around us.

Artists believe in themselves. That's all. They think it's okay to like what they like, and to share what they like with others. Believing in yourself and sharing it with the world. That's what makes an artist.

Weaver Finch on Artists

Come gather round and I'll tell you a story.

My grandfather was a woodcarver. I'd like you to hear about the cedar salmon he carved.

My grandfather lived in the San Juan Islands. He could've taken a ferry to his home, but he preferred going to and from the mainland in his own wooden boat. As he'd chug through the channel, he watched the dark waters for salmon. My grandfather assured us, if he really wanted to spot salmon, he would hike up the rivers where the salmon spawned. But he wasn't interested in counting lots of salmon. What thrilled my grandfather was seeing the salmon out in salt water. He never knew why, but his stomach would flip when he spotted his first salmon of the year. His old eyes twinkled as he watched the silvery flash of their tails when they jumped.

continued

Weaver Finch on Artists

(continued)

On calm days my grandfather would turn off the motor, and let his boat float. The currents in the San Juans were swift. He couldn't leave the motor off long, as he'd soon be heading out to sea. He would drift as long as he dared, imagining the fish swimming in the boat beneath him. My grandfather told me he liked the quiet, as then he could feel what it might be like to be a salmon in those deep waters.

One week, Grandfather didn't cross the channel to town. The wind was blowing with a terrible howl. But it wasn't the storm that kept him home. Grandfather lived next to a seaward creek. A great tree, one that had stood tall since Grandfather was a boy, had fallen in the storm.

My grandfather spent days by the cedar tree. He touched it. He smelled it. He sat among the fallen limbs until he could almost see his salmon in the wood. That's how Grandfather talked about carving. He would picture an animal inside his head, but he'd wait to begin carving until he saw clearly how that animal was positioned in a particular piece. Then he'd simply carve away any of the wood that wasn't the animal.

To carve a school of salmon in a fallen tree, Grandfather first had to strip away all the bark and take off most of the limbs. Then he sat with the tree awhile longer to spot each and every salmon.

When he finally began, it took Grandfather days and weeks of pounding a wooden mallet onto his chisel. He'd hold the chisel tight, and pound and pound, slicing at an angle in one spot, chipping straight in at another. He worked so long, the mallet and the chisel became like parts of his hands. He said it felt strange to set them down at night.

Slowly, slowly, new life appeared in the fallen tree. Yes. My grandfather carved six great silver salmon, Coho they call them, in the top half of that old cedar. At first the salmon were rough. But Grandfather rasped and sandpapered until the salmons' backs were completely smooth. That took almost as much time as the carving. Then he rubbed oil into the wood. That made the sun glint off their fins. The salmon looked like they were swimming. My grandfather rested. He was happy with his work.

Finch, three, two, one. This story is done.

Astronaut

Space Shuttle

Construct a space shuttle out of an oblong of cardboard boxes, stacked two high.

Let children attach heat resistant tiles all over the outside. The tiles can be made out of cardboard, taped in layers like roofing.

Use two oatmeal boxes, stacked on each side, or one ice cream drum, at either side of the shuttle, for boosters.

Make control center panel by affixing gadgets onto a flat cardboard.

Space Station

space station—large wooden blocks

space packs—pillow case filled with small blanket, belted on space helmets—(see project on page 90) Tape these to the pack with a plastic tubing, simulating life-support system.

space suits—If possible, borrow clean coveralls from some other profession. If not, have children don long-sleeved sweatshirts allotted to the play. Have children stuff tissue or towels inside their "suits" after they put them on. Rubber band their wrists and ankles.

cord—Pin something like a bathrobe cord onto the suit. The cord can be taped to the blocks, for "working off the station."

Space Helmets

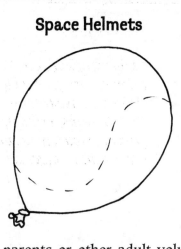

 Ask parents or other adult volunteers to blow up large-size balloons, and tie.

Do not allow preschool children to blow up their own balloons; balloons are a choking hazard. Do not use this activity unless you are right there with the children so you can be sure no children put the balloons in their mouths.

Using a marker, draw a line around the balloon, as shown (exposing face and neck).

Let the children dip strips of newspaper in liquid starch to cover the top part of the helmet, several layers thick. You can cut a hole in the top of a cardboard box, just smaller than the bottom third of the balloon, to hold the balloon while working.

 When dry, children pop the balloon. *An adult* needs to cut away the lower part of the balloon.

The helmets can be painted however the children want.

In Space

Space, space,   *(Arms reaching out.)*
floating out in space.   *(Slowly turn from side to side.)*
Floating,   *(Reach arms straight ahead.)*
Falling,   *(Pull in arms, crumple to a squat.)*
Rolling,   *(Turn completely around, squatting still.)*
Crawling.   *(Crawl, in exaggerated, slow motion.)*
Space, space,
Space.

Repeat.
Repeat again, balancing balloons.

Moons

Let children pat out their own biscuits (prepared or homemade dough).
Let children cut or mold into a moon shape.

Bake as directed. Be sure *an adult* puts the pans in and out of the oven.
Dip in "moonlight." (blended cream cheese and vanilla pudding).

Game

Crew, Return to Ship

Have children scatter all over room, gym, or designated outdoor area.

Demonstrate moon leap (jump-walk, slow motion).

Have children try one leap. Repeat.

The point of the game is to get all the crew back to the ship.

Set a box in the middle of the group. That is the space ship.

Have six cards. Boldly number 1 to 6, one number on a card, with the corresponding number of large dots on each.

The leader draws a card, and holds it up, calling out the number. All children (crew) take that many moon leaps towards the ship.

The leader draws another card and repeats until all in the crew are back to the ship.

When everyone gets back, the leader picks a replacement, and at the new leader's command "Explore," the children scatter.

When the leader says "Crew return to ship," they freeze. Then, as in the first round, each time the leader holds up a card, calling out a number, the crew get to moon leap that many steps back to the ship.

The game is over when everyone has had a turn being leader.

Weaver Finch on Space

Come gather round and I'll tell you a story.

Last week I dreamt I was in a space shuttle. I was one of the astronauts. Imagine! And you were there _____, and _____, and _____ (name everyone sitting around the room).

We were all buckled in (everyone buckle safety belts). Mission control had checked and double checked. All systems were "go." We could hear the Commander counting down: 10, 9, 8, _____, _____, _____, _____, _____, _____, _____!

There was a rumble (make loud rumbles).
And a shaking (shaking selves).
And the shuttle left the ground.

Our faces were pushed back (look up, pressing hands on cheeks as if moving against great pressure).

We were going up and up (everybody stand).
Finally we were soaring out through space.
The commander said "Ready for space walk."

We unbuckled our safety belts (unbuckle), put on our life support systems (pretend to put on packs and helmets, with hose connecting), attached our cords (pretend connecting waist to "space shuttle" or chair). Then we went out the hatch, and (hold hands, pretend to float) walked in space.

There were stars in every direction. It was wondrous. (Still holding hands, form a circle; walk whole group around in a circle, then back through same pretend door, to sit down.) We went back into the space shuttle, closed the shuttle door, and BOOM! (clap hands) I woke up.

Finch, three, two, one. This story is done.

Baker

Baking

Buns.	*(Stand up.)*
Buns.	*(Squat.)*
Buns.	*(Stand up.)*
Buns.	*(Squat.)*
Cinnamon buns for sale!	*(Stand up, arms held high, palms up.)*
Cakes.	*(March in place.)*
Cakes.	
Cakes.	
Cakes.	
Fancy decorated cakes!	*(Pump right hand up and down, as with a baton.)*
Muffins.	*(Hop, turning in a circle.)*
Muffins.	
Muffins.	
Muffins.	
Plump blueberry muffins!	*(Hands move together and apart, from front to sides.)*

Bakers Make Healthy Granola

1 C. chopped dried fruit, unsweetened
3/4 C. honey
1/2 can nonfat condensed milk
1/2 tsp. vanilla
1/4 C. oil
4 C. rolled oats
1 C. wheat germ
1 C. rolled rye
1 C. sunflower seeds, raw
1 C. nuts, chopped

Mix wet ingredients together. Pour over dry ingredients. Stir.

Spread on cookie sheet. Bake at 350 degrees for 1 hour.

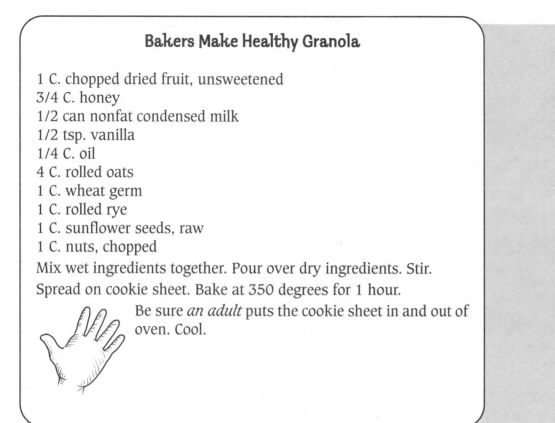 Be sure *an adult* puts the cookie sheet in and out of oven. Cool.

Playdough Bakers

Expand playdough fun by adding recycled pot pie tins, a large bag of marbles, plastic markers such as Tiddlywinks, and circles of cardboard. Sounds like pepperoni pizza and cherry pie to me, but there's no telling what your children will make!

(Be sure to take into account the ages of your children. Don't put out marbles or other small objects if your children still put things in their mouths.)

Activity

Gingerbread Cookies

1 stick margarine, room temperature
1/2 C. honey
1/2 C. molasses
1 egg
1 Tbsp. vinegar
1 C. whole wheat flour
2 C. unbleached flour
1 1/4 tsp. baking soda
1/2 tsp. salt
1 tsp. mace or ginger

Mix wet ingredients. Stir into dry ingredients, blending well.

Chill for at least 1 hour.

Roll out on clean, lightly floured surface.

Each child cuts a gingerbread person.

Place on greased cookie sheet. Sprinkle with a very little bit of raw or granulated sugar. Bake 375 degree oven, 7 to 8 minutes.

 Be sure *an adult* puts the cookie sheet in and out of the oven. Let cool.

If you have vegans in your group (vegans don't eat or use animal products), substitute raw sugar for the honey, and a banana for the egg. The non-vegans won't notice a difference in taste. And without eggs, you won't have to keep children from nibbling on the dough.

At snack time, pretend you're at the bakery. Draw names, or in some other way choose two bakers and a shopkeeper. The bakers bring the cookies out front to the display table. The shopkeeper sells the cookies to the rest of the class (customers) for pretend money. You could elaborate with a cashier collecting tokens to put in a cash box or cash register.

Rolls

Using prepared biscuit dough, let each child form
bow knot
layers
or clover leaf

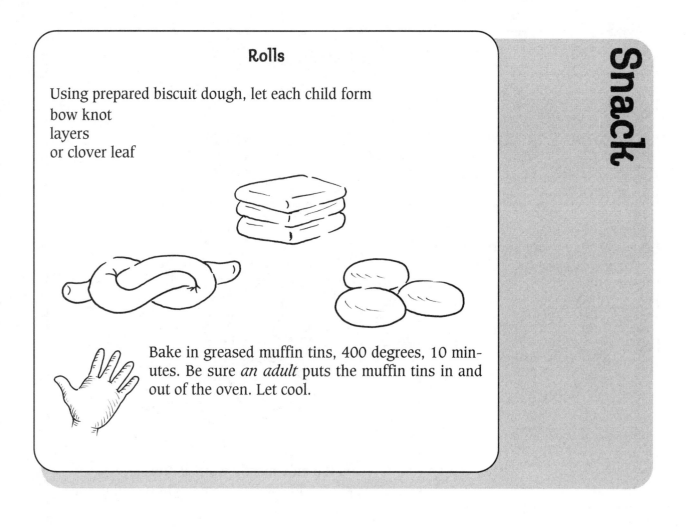

Bake in greased muffin tins, 400 degrees, 10 minutes. Be sure *an adult* puts the muffin tins in and out of the oven. Let cool.

Weaver Finch on Baking

Come gather round and I'll tell you a story.

When I was growing up, children ate a lot of sweets. Most children had to work very hard. Besides going to school, children who lived in the country had to clean out the barn or work in the garden. Children in the city had to sweep walks or sell newspapers every afternoon. They liked sweet treats after working so hard.

Why, I remember one autumn, it was the yearly harvest party in my hometown. All the families for miles around drove to the Hall with their trucks and trunks full of apples. The community cider press had the place of honor on the wide back porch. The men took turns feeding the hoppers and turning the crank to make apple cider.

When I was a girl, women worked indoors and the men mostly worked outside. Nowadays some men might help with the baking, and some women might turn the cider press, but not back then.

So in the year that I'm telling you about, the women all worked in the kitchen. They had mixed up huge batches of doughnut batter. Several volunteered to roll and cut the doughnuts on big tables laid out with pastry cloths. Others stood by the stove beside vats of boiling oil. The cooks dropped the circles of dough into the oil, waiting until just the right second to pull the puffy doughnuts out with long-handled tongs. Finally, another couple of volunteers shook the doughnuts in brown bags of sugar.

Hot doughnuts and cold apple cider! Folks in my hometown sure loved the harvest party. The children kept coming back for more. Finally the cooks had to set a limit on the number of doughnuts the children could eat.

The whole town was full, everyone that is, except the fiddlers, who'd been busy all night playing music for the party. Finally at half past ten, everyone, except the fiddlers, rolled on home. The fiddlers stayed and ate a big stack of doughnuts themselves.

Finch, three, two, one. This story is done.

City Planner

Plan a City

Designate a protected area on the floor, a table top, or a large sheet of cardboard. Talk about "city limits."

Discuss what's in a city or town. (houses, apartments, office buildings, factories, green spaces, parks, roads, cars, etc.)

What will they need to build a model of a city? (blocks, bricks, building sets such as Legos, cardboard, colored construction paper, crayons, small cars, train set, etc.)

Trees can be made of toilet paper tubes, adorned with thin strips of curled construction paper.

Let this be a several day or several week activity. Set ground rules that people can work together, but they cannot take down or change something someone else has built without asking.

Variation:

Collect small boxes, plastic bottles, papers, cardboard. Let each child make her own city, using materials that can be taken home.

One easy way to organize this project is to let each child build a miniature city on an upside-down cardboard box. As all the cities sprout up, they become a mini-metropolis. Encourage children to visit each other, to share ideas and help each other out.

Snack

City

Set out a tray with:

cheese cubes for buildings
crackers for streets
sprouts for grass
grapes for flowers (cut X on top of each)
celery sticks for trees (sliver the tops; stand in cream cheese)

Project

City Park and Playground Mural

construction paper rectangles for houses surrounding the park
color crayons for drawing playground equipment
recycled shredded grass (from spring decorations)
construction paper trees

Project

City of the Future

Talk with the children about how the world changes, what we rely on now that was not even conceived of when our grandparents were children. If you give very specific examples, the children will understand and have fun exploring this idea with you. For instance, I might say, "When my Grandma was a very little girl, her family had no telephone." "When my mom was a little girl, TV's hadn't been invented. No one had a TV."

Can your children imagine what cities might look like when they are as old as their grandparents? Talk about plastic recycling, and how posts and beams can now be made out of recycled milk cartons. And how walls can be made out of mud and straw (straw bale construction). And so on.

Possible themes for constructing a future city:

recycled plastic city (collect materials so you have plenty to match the children's imaginations)
underground city (perhaps best made outdoors)
city in the clouds (tissue paper and cotton balls)
ideas that your children come up with

Skippety on City Planning

Let's make the buildings
not so tall.

Let's make pictures
on the walls.

How about swing sets
at the bus stop?

How about bird posts
with feeders on top?

Don't forget pathways
through the city
where we can walk dogs,
all brushed and pretty.

Say, how about moving
the streets underground
so there wouldn't be noisy
traffic all around?

I think it'd be nice
to have flowers everywhere
with a law that says
you can pick *one* for your hair.

How about a squirrels'
jungle gym?

With an elevator up
so we can pet them?

Planning the city
sounds like fun.

I think the children
could help get it done.

Weaver Finch on City Planning

Come gather round and I'll tell you a story.

Once I visited a city where they needed a planner like you, and you, and you. That city was a mess.

The downtown was way too crowded. People had trouble getting past each other on the sidewalks, and crossing the street was almost impossible. The cars hardly stopped, even when people were in the crosswalk. I had special trouble because of my wheelchair. Some places there was no ramp off the curb, so I had to bump, bump down, hoping I wouldn't lose my balance. I didn't want to tip over into the street.

Getting around in the city was hard, but at least I got to go home at the end of my visit.

The people who lived right in the city, the ones who didn't have much money, had to live in old falling-down apartment buildings, either that or live on the street. There was garbage in the alleys and litter all over the sidewalks.

I was wondering what you would do if you were asked to help. Pretend one day you answer the phone and it is someone from the City Council. The City Council are women and men who keep everything working in a town or a city. What if the City Council wanted to know your opinion about how to make the downtown a better place? What would you say?

City Planner _____ (child's name)?

(Possible questions:

What would you change? What would you make new?

Where would you get the money?

How would the changes help the people who live downtown?

What about the plants and animals? How would you help them?

Make the discussion fun. Stop whenever they lose interest.)

You can see, there's a lot to think about when planning changes downtown. City Planners work hard for all of us.

Finch, three, two, one. This story is done.

Construction Worker

City Outdoors

Gather large to medium-size cardboard boxes.

Set a ground rule: "City ordinance says buildings may be only three boxes high."

Let three or four children work together to build a city, with buildings separated to accommodate roads for big wheels and trikes. Have the children measure to be sure the buildings are more than two vehicle widths apart.

The children can use wagons to carry the "lumber."

Cut doors and windows where children request them. Add cardboard window boxes. The children can decorate the buildings, as desired.

Let each new group of children add to the city, or move buildings to meet new needs.

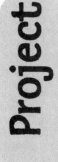

Project

Milk Carton Towers

You'll have to collect quite a number of cartons for this to be interesting.

Designate a floor area that won't be disrupted for a few days.

Children can stack milk cartons, using masking tape to hold the towers together. Construction paper can be cut and taped on for roofs, doors, and windows.

Variation: juice can towers

Frozen juice containers make good material for a table-size version of tower building. Buildings can be stuck together with paste or masking tape.

Try a single sheet of newspaper, rolled tight, with ends taped together, and bent into a triangle, for added variety in construction forms.

Project

Log House

Make logs by rolling two sheets of newspaper in a tight roll.

Fit one end inside the other. Tape.

Walls are made by forming one roll into a rectangle. Cut a shorter piece and tape corner to corner in diagonal, for strength.

Use short rolls for interior uprights at corners.

Fold a rectangle of construction paper for roof.

Tape together and paint, if desired.

Cob Houses

If you work with children in a rural area, you may have sufficient dirt and straw to make miniature cob houses.

Gather straw.

Mix straw with dirt.

Add water only until materials adhere.

Pack mixture into individual milk containers.

Let dry.

Peel the containers off the "bricks."

Let children use them for building a house, sticking the bricks together with glue or a mud paste.

If you have Internet access, show children real cob buildings. For example, check out http://www.cpros.com/~sequoia/ or do a search for the many other web sites on cob building or other alternative construction.

Structures

Collect a box full of paper towel and toilet paper tubes.

Make slits about an inch deep into the tubes at both ends.

Children can make bridges and overpasses by fitting one tube into the slits of another. Connect with flattened tubes, taped to uprights.

For added involvement, bring out paints and long-handled poster paint brushes.

When dry, the children can use their structures with mini-cars, for play.

Skippety on Building

Rickety tip,
No building of mine
Will tippety tip.

I'll take the time.

I'll build it straight.

I'll build it tall.

I'll build the happiest
Buildings of all.

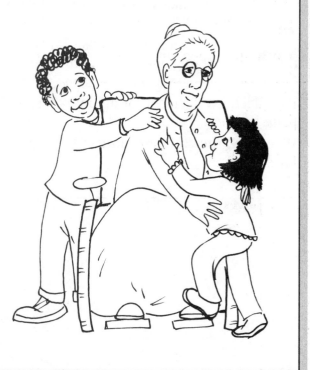

Weaver Finch on Building

Come gather round and I'll tell you a story.

Once there was a woman with a small white house. She loved her little house. The hummingbirds came to her porch and drank nectar from the fuchsias. The woman had three children though. As the children grew, the woman decided she needed to add more rooms.

The woman had one son. His name was _____. He helped his mom plan how to build the rooms. He and his friend, _____, went to the library for books on building. The woman had a daughter named _____. She and her friend, _____, helped with the house design. Together the family and their friends made a cardboard model of the old part of

Weaver Finch on Building
(continued)

their house and how it would look after they added on. Finally they got a permit and were ready to begin.

The woman called in the excavators. (Alternate, girls and boys' names from your group for the workers in this story.) Their names were _____ and _____. They dug trenches for the foundation walls. Then the concrete workers arrived. _____, _____, and _____ pulled up with the big cement trucks. They poured cement for the foundation.

Next her son helped the carpenters, _____, _____, and _____. They framed up the walls. Then the carpenters put in the windows. Next came the siders, _____ and _____, who put boards on the outside of the new part of the house. The roofers, _____ and _____, hammered the shingles on the roof. Then the sheet rockers, _____ and _____, arrived to put up the inside walls. The plumber, _____, put in the pipes and hooked up the sink, the washing machine, and the new toilet. The electrician, _____, put in all the new wiring and lights.

Finally the son, the daughter, and the mother painted the inside of their addition. They sang a painting song while they worked.

The whole outside of their home had become a mess though. The workers had left scraps of building materials lying in the yard. Sadly, they had also crushed the fuchsia bushes. So when the oldest daughter, _____, came home from college, she helped smooth the ground and plant new flowers all around the house. She planted a whole border of lupine by the driveway too. Before long the family had lots of friends stopping by to see all their new rooms. Everyone loved the house, inside and out.

Finch, three, two, one. This story is done.

Farmer

Snack

Farmer's Pocket Biscuits

Have the child you're acknowledging help you prepare the vegetables. If the child is older, she can chop carrots. A preschooler with average development can chop celery with a table knife. A younger preschooler can break pieces of spinach into small bits. The child can set these out in separate bowls along with a bowl of frozen peas.

Give each child two prepared biscuit dough rounds. As the bowls of farm food are passed, the children put little bits onto one biscuit. Poking in the vegetables will flatten the biscuit. Then they add a pat of butter and a sprinkle of dried herb, such as parsley or basil. The remaining biscuit is set on top of the first and patted down. The children pinch the edges together, so the vegetables are pocketed inside.

Make a map of the cookie sheet as the children place on their pocket biscuits so you can match the snacks back to their makers.

Bake on a greased cookie sheet, at 400 degrees for 10 minutes.

 Be sure *an adult* puts the cookie sheets in and out of the oven. Cool.

Skippety on Farming

Cabbage, turnips,
Corn and peas.

Huckleberries.

Apples on trees.

Sweet potatoes,
Lima beans.

Watermelon,
Spinach greens.

Hazelnuts and
Grapes and beets.

Farmers grow us
Tasty treats.

Farming

Fill up a water table or other container with dirt. Offer:
tractor, trailer, trucks
farm animals
small figures
beans or dried peas for "planting" (See below.)
bits of dry grass
little twigs

Farm play comes alive when we add "seeds" to plant, hay for the animals, and little bits of rocks or twigs for building materials.

Of course you will be sure to offer this activity only to children who are developmentally beyond putting small items in their mouths.

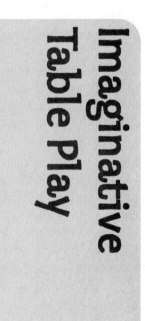

Imaginative Table Play

Planting

Slice brown bread.

Pass butter and hulled sunflower seeds. Let children plant their seeds in rows.

Warm, and eat.

Farmer's Garden

Here's a way of recycling all those jeans cuffs we cut off for hemming:

First of all, go a'gathering with your group, bringing back dried grasses and other dried plants and seed pods. If you have an abundance of flowering weeds, allow the children to pick these as well.

Back at your tables, give each child a small circle of brown construction paper.

Pass out cut-off jeans cuffs.

Have the children set the cuff in a stand-up circle on their paper, and drizzle glue around the outside bottom edge.

With the glue already in place, let the children create their own stand-up garden in the round, by sticking their gathered treasures around the edge of the cuff.

Of course, the children may come up with another way to assemble the materials. Be sure to let them.

Weaver Finch on Farming

Come gather round and I'll tell you a story.

Once there was an old woman who lived on a farm way up on a road, the other side of Wauconda. In the summer, the lilac bushes around her house were full of purple and white blossoms. Such an ice-cream-sweet smell; made you want to bury your face in the bushes!

The old woman had a small herd of dairy cows. Well, four to be exact. All summer, morning and night, she trudged out to the barn in her black rubber boots. The woman rang the bell. Then she waited for her cows to mosey in to be milked. Once a day, her daughter who ran the Wauconda Store came by to pick up the fresh milk.

The old woman said, "You mustn't take time from your store like this to be running up here every day. The milk'll keep."

But the daughter wouldn't mind her. She kept coming for the milk every day.

Then one day late in the summer, the daughter didn't show up. The old woman thought, "Finally, she's going to listen to me!" But the next day the daughter didn't come either.

The old woman pulled on her big black rubber boots, strapped two milk jugs to the ends of a pole, put the pole over her shoulders, and started down the windy road to the Wauconda Store. It was nearly nightfall by the time the old woman rounded the last bend. And what do you think she saw? _____

(If your children have trouble finishing this one, get them started with, a pile of logs in front of the daughter's car, or a passel of puppies in a box by the door. Then ask, how do you suppose the logs or puppies got there?)

Finch, three, two, one. This story is done.

Fast Food Service Worker

Project

Submarine Sandwich Making

Wrap both the top and bottom of egg cartons in tissue so the carton can still be opened, resembling a submarine sandwich. Tape to hold the tissue in place.

Have a selection of "fillings" available, such as:

scraps of cloth

pieces of cardboard

paper pieces, cut in rounds

crinkled pieces of tissue paper

Let the children spread on a light glue and water mixture with their own plastic knives. They then select and assemble their "submarine sandwiches."

When the glue has dried, help the children set up a Sub Shop, where they can pretend to sell the sandwiches, taking turns as shop keeper, customers, and hungry families back home.

Project

Hats

Make fast-food worker hats out of colored construction paper. Color striped edges, dots on top, or whatever design the children choose.

Burger Drive-in

Use burger baskets such as found in drive-ins (I located some in a church rummage sale) or berry baskets from the grocers. You can also make baskets out of the bottom four inches of medium-size paper bags, cut off. Turn down the tops of the bag, for strength.

Other items you'll want for pretend play:

tall plastic cups

ice cream maker (Label a large cardboard box. Make a lever by fitting a piece of cardboard into a slot cut in front. A spout can be made out of inserting a toilet paper tube into a hole cut in the front, two spouts for two flavors.)

paper cones, to approximate ice cream cones (Children can tape paper triangles into cones, and stack them as in a drive-in).

cash register and play money

pad of paper and pencil

circles of cardboard of two different weights, for hamburgers and buns

recycled tissue paper, for wrapping buns

Vegetarians can play "Garden Burgers."

Outdoor Variation

Set up fast food kitchen outdoors.

Establish a drive-up window.

Assemble trikes and big wheels.

Add recycled take-out bags to your restaurant supplies.

Set up an outdoor eating area or park near the restaurant, including a parking lot and garbage/recycling bins.

Skippety on Fast Food Restaurants

Chicken burger, pizza,
maybe French fries.
Hamburger, chocolate shake,
medium-size.

Fish fillet, coleslaw,
biscuits and potatoes.
Double cheeseburger
with pickles and tomatoes.

Now for dessert:
a triple duper sundae,
and a special freeze fudge
served any day but Monday.

Add seven iced yogurts,
each with a topping.
After all this sweet stuff
I'm bound to be a'hopping!

Snack

Mini Tacos

Heat mini tortillas in oven (or use regular size, cut in half).
Have children chop up tomatoes and lettuce.

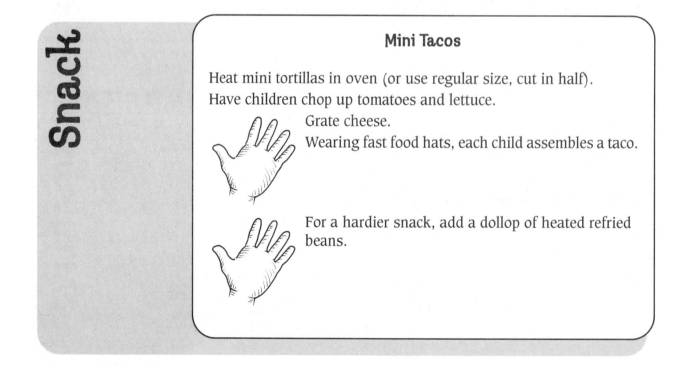

Grate cheese.
Wearing fast food hats, each child assembles a taco.

For a hardier snack, add a dollop of heated refried beans.

Weaver Finch on Fast Food Restaurants

Come gather round and I'll tell you a story.

Once, I remember, I owned a drive-in restaurant. That restaurant was a cheery place. All the workers wore yellow outfits. I wore yellow stretch pants, high-top sneakers, and a yellow sweater with the words . . . oh dear, I've forgotten. It was such a long time ago. What do you suppose was the name of my restaurant? _____ _____

I'm sure it was one of those names. And my sweater had the name sewn right on the front.

I remember we served cabbage mustard soup, but I can't remember what else was on the menu. What do you suppose the customers came in to order? _____, _____, _____, etc.

If you owned a restaurant, what would you serve? _____ (etc.) I'd come to eat at your restaurant.

Finch, three, two, one. This story is done.

Firefighter

Ceremony for Bravery

Talk with the children about what it means to be brave, what it means to be a hero. Talk about how heroes stay strong and do their jobs, even when they're afraid. You don't need to bring up horrific national events. If the children do mention such news, go ahead and talk with them about the firefighters' or police officers' role in rescues. They may bring up firefighting or rescues they've heard of in your community. Take your clues from the children's experience. Don't scare them with information to which they haven't already been exposed.

Talk about honoring. How do we show a firefighter our appreciation for putting out a fire or for saving someone's life? Add the children's ideas about a ceremony to the imaginative fire fighting play.

You might want to put the pretend firefighters' pictures on a poster. Or let the children make an award out of construction paper. The children can design what signifies heartfelt appreciation for them. Smiley faces? Gold stars? Let them decide.

If you have had an actual event in your community, let the children make awards to send to the real firefighters. Or take a trip to your local firehouse to let the children deliver the appreciations in person.

Firefighting Training

Set a long straight ladder on the ground.

Let children practice walking between rungs.

Set the ladder off the ground about 4" (on large, sturdy wooden blocks).

Let the children practice crawling across.

Add walking on a balance beam.

Make an obstacle course including all of these physical training exercises.

Firefighting

Firehouse:

play kitchen for food preparation

pretend beds for rest

nerf basketball hoop for exercise

Garage:

big wheels and wagons for fire trucks

wrapping paper tubes for fire hoses

check boxes from bank for walkie talkies

rope for rescues

cereal box for first aid kit

oatmeal box for oxygen tank

any hard hats for helmets

Community Aide

Often during holidays or in response to families who have suffered a fire, local fire departments collect canned goods, used clothing, or furniture, which they distribute to the families in need.

Depending on the circumstances of the children in your group, either have them bring items from home, or help them make a toy such as a sock puppet or doll clothes to take to the fire department for the next drive. Let the children be the givers.

continued

Community Aide
(continued)

Sock-puppet materials:
socks, used, without holes
buttons for eyes
small bits of felt for nose and mouth
Older children can use plastic, blunt-tipped darning needles and embroidery thread for sewing on the buttons. A parent or volunteer can sew for the younger ones in your group.
Children can glue on the felt features.

Winger on Firefighting

"Here I come! Here I come! I'll save you!" Fire-fighters talk like that. They are brave men and women who care about other people.

If I was a firefighter I'd fly really fast to get to the people in trouble. If people were in a fire or in a wreck, I'd help them get out.

Have you ever seen firefighters put out a fire? Have you ever seen firefighters help with a rescue?

If you know a firefighter, or have a firefighter in your family, you can be very glad. Helping people is a big part of a firefighter's job.

We can give the firefighters a hand. Do you know how to prevent fires? (Do you know what *prevent* means? It means to keep a fire from happening.)
We're talking serious, aren't we? Fire is serious. Here are some things we have to remember so we can keep fires from happening:
Matches are not for play. *Always* give matches and lighters to an adult.
Let your parent or guardian use the stove or oven. Never do cooking by yourself.
Candles are for adults and special occasions. Tell an adult if you see a child using matches or candles.

Winger on Firefighting
(continued)

We can help prevent people from getting hurt in fires too.

Talk with your family about smoke alarms. Do you have enough smoke alarms and are the batteries working? If not, let me know. We can get you new batteries.

Also, be sure you have a meeting spot outside your home so if there ever is a fire, you and your family can meet up at a safe spot.

One way to remember these safety tips is to tell them to sisters or brothers or other people who are younger than you.

Weaver Finch on Firefighting

Come gather round and I'll tell you a story.

Once when I lived in the city, I rented an apartment that was several stories up. If you live in a house with no stairs in it, you might have to imagine what my apartment was like. When I lived there, I could still walk. I would walk up almost three-hundred stairs just to get to my apartment.

Early one morning the smoke alarms in the hallway started to go off. I heard scuffling, then running and shouting. I hurried out of my bedroom, and went right to the front door, but I didn't open it because I could see smoke seeping in underneath. I grabbed a blanket off the back of the couch, and pushed it up against the bottom of the door.

Then I hurried to the kitchen and closed the door behind me. I went to the window and climbed out onto the fire escape. The fire escape was a metal platform outside the breakfast nook window. I made sure to close that window behind me. I just had on my pajamas, so it was cold out on the fire escape. I hoped someone would help me from there. Even as I was climbing out, I saw the fire trucks coming down the street, flashing their lights. Do you know how the lights go, round and round?

continued

Weaver Finch on Firefighting
(continued)

In just a minute, the fire truck was underneath our apartment building. The firefighters had ladders up against the apartment wall. Some firefighters were helping the people on the top floors. They were climbing down on ladders that rested against the fire escapes above me. Other firefighters were going in the main doors down below. Smoke poured out, but I couldn't see any flames.

Before long it was my turn to climb out on that tall ladder. I was very scared, but a firefighter was right underneath me. When I looked down my legs got all shaky, but the firefighter held onto me so I wouldn't slip and fall. When I got down to the fire engine and then onto the ground, I helped hold my neighbor's children who were already safe. We waited and waited for almost an hour.

The firefighters figured that someone must have put a cigarette into a trash bin. A smoldering smoky fire had started in the basement. The smoke went up through the furnace vents from floor to floor, but the fire was still just in that one basement room. The firefighters sprayed water to put out the fire.

We were lucky. Because of the firefighters, no one was hurt. A cafe across the street invited all the people from the apartment building to come in and get warm. They gave us hot cocoa and coffee. We got to talk to friends in our building as the firefighters finished their work. Several hours later we were allowed back in our apartments. It smelled smoky in the halls still, but my apartment was just fine.

I'll always remember those dear firefighters and the good work they did that early morning.

Has anyone else been in a fire? Do you want to tell us about it? _____

Finch, three, two, one. This story is done.

Garbage
Collector/
Recycler

Caring for Our World

Purchase thin rubber gloves, such as used for house painting, for you and the children. (It's okay for the children to know simply that some garbage can be dangerous.) If drug needles are a concern in your area though, *do not involve the children in clean-up.*

Begin each month by picking up around your area, your school yard or block.

Reuse/Recycle

The process, the social or tactile experience, the creativity, or the practice with large and small muscle coordination outweigh the importance of the product in most early childhood activities. Yet so many school projects inevitably result in products. Parents will appreciate your setting up a display area where they may view the work of the week, making decisions at school about which pieces should go home.

Turns can be taken for the ongoing job of disassembling projects, sorting whatever is recyclable or reusable, and throwing the rest away. Add this activity to your list of assigned jobs.

Skippety on Cutting Down on Garbage

I think again
'fore I throw things away.

Skip doo de oo la
Skip doo de ay.

Stuff could be reused
recycled, I say.

Skip doo de oo lee ay.

Composting, bulk buying,
Making less trash.

Skip doo de oo la
Skip doo de ay.

I do my part
to help our earth last.

Skip doo de oo lee ay!

Composting

Your ability to construct and use a compost bin will, of course, depend on your locale. If you're in a city setting, composting may not be feasible, although many cities now have community garden plots. You might work out an arrangement for a volunteer from a neighborhood garden to come by and pick up your compost if you can't create a system for your own use. If you are able to use your own composting, let children help you construct a frame.

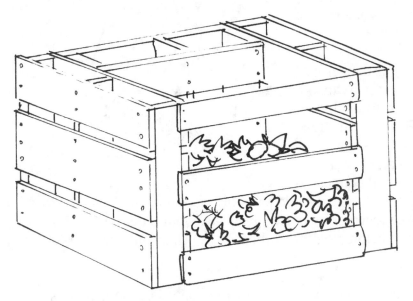

three 3′ × 3′ pallets from a furniture store
three 3′ long two-by-fours
nails

The children can compost fruit and vegetable scraps from their snack preparation, adding a sprinkling of dirt over the top.

Every week or so, let them turn the pile, adding a little dirt.

After the bin is two-thirds full, let it sit for several months. Then you can use this composted dirt for planting with the children.

Winger on Garbage

I think a lot about garbage. We can have less garbage, you know.

I suppose you do recycling with your families. Recycle. That means turning in things that you've already used to be made over again into something new. Like, old cans can be recycled and made into new cans. We can recycle plastic, glass, paper, and cardboard. Recycling saves energy and makes our world a prettier place.

Did you know some garbage is dangerous? The plastic circles that connect pop cans together can be bad for birds. Birds find them in garbage dumps, or when they're washed up on the beaches. Birds can accidentally get their heads stuck in the plastic circles. Then they can't fly or eat, so they die. If I got my head stuck in one, I could probably get out or call for help. But birds can't. If you buy pop hooked together by those circles, ask your parent or guardian to help you cut the circles apart before you throw them away. That could be your job, to help the birds.

Then there are balloons. Did you know you should wrap popped balloons up in some other garbage, before you throw them away? That way birds won't see the bright balloon and try to eat it. If a bird eats a balloon, the bird will choke and maybe die. We want to be careful not to let balloons sail away up in the sky either, because when they break and fall to earth, birds or other animals might try to eat them.

There's a lot to think about when it comes to garbage. What do you think about garbage?

Weaver Finch on Service

Come gather round and I'll tell you a story.

Once upon a time there was a garbage collector. He was strong. He had to be. Every week he lifted hundreds of garbage cans and dumped them into his truck.

Besides being strong, Cal was probably the kindest man in town. As he went around town hauling away people's garbage, he gave good cheer to anyone who would take it. He would smile and wave at the children going by in the school bus. He'd smile and wave to the moms or dads as they walked their little ones to the park. He took extra time picking up older people's garbage right at their door. And he'd stop to chat for a minute too. Then he'd work faster to make up time. By afternoon, he'd still have a wave and a grin for the teenagers getting out of school. Cal made his job special. And he made everyone on his route feel brighter too.

Cal reminds me of another worker, a flagger on a bridge repair site. Her job was to hold out a sign to stop cars and trucks while workers repaired the bridge. The flagger's name was Lisa; I'll always remember Lisa too.

It didn't matter how windy or rainy it got, Lisa had a smile and a wave for everyone. Sometimes I'd see her early in the morning, and then again on my way home. Even late in the day Lisa would still be waving and smiling to the drivers. That flagger made her job special, and she made everyone who passed by feel a little bit brighter too.

Do you know a really friendly person like Cal or Lisa? _____ Tell us about who you know. What does that person do to make the world brighter?

Finch, three, two, one. This story is done.

Hair Stylist

Note:
Besides acknowledging a child whose family member works as a hair stylist, these activities will serve as a positive follow-up to a child's cutting his own hair. You may want to share ideas with the parent, so she too can offer constructive alternatives.

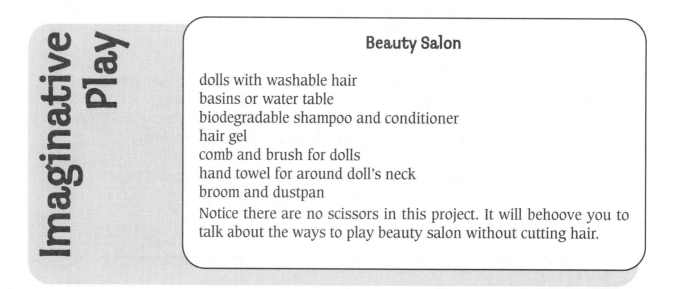

Imaginative Play

Beauty Salon

dolls with washable hair
basins or water table
biodegradable shampoo and conditioner
hair gel
comb and brush for dolls
hand towel for around doll's neck
broom and dustpan

Notice there are no scissors in this project. It will behoove you to talk about the ways to play beauty salon without cutting hair.

Box Heads

Each child will have a thin cardboard box (e.g., Kleenex box).

Draw circles on construction paper, the width of the boxes.

The children stand their box on end. They can glue the circles on for a face, then draw on features. If the cardboard is flimsy enough, toothpicks can be stuck into the top of the boxes for hair. Or a thin piece of styrofoam can be glued to the top of the box, into which children can easily poke toothpicks.

Some children will want to paint or color their hair with magic markers.

Alternate hair ideas: yarn or wrapping ribbon

Project

Pretend Hair Cutting

Trace around a child's upper body on a large piece of cardboard. If you have a large enough cardboard, trace the entire body. Cut out the figure.

Children will help with features and clothing. They can also glue or tape on pieces of yarn for hair.

Sit the cut-out up in a chair (bending at waist, if full-length), and tie to chair with an apron if necessary.

Children can perform the haircut.

Put on new yarn. Repeat, until everyone who wants has had a turn.

Caution the children that this is not a project they should do on real people. If you care for children who will not take heed, skip pretend hair cutting altogether.

Activity

People

Peel and cut kiwi fruit in half lengthwise.

Snack helpers will set halves on individual plates.

Using sunflower seeds for features and alfalfa sprouts for hair, snack helpers can make faces.

Variations: Use Cheerios for eyes and apple slices for mouths.

Snack

Project

Heads

Let the children trace around large pot lids, to make circles on construction paper.

Let the children put on features with unusual equipment:

Using wind-fallen sprigs of evergreen boughs for brushes the children can paint hair on their heads. Offer choices of paint colors and different kinds of boughs, to simulate differences.

The children may want to glue on other natural materials such as twigs, cones, or lichen for the eyes, nose, and mouth, or they can draw on the features.

Use chalk or natural materials for blush and lipstick.

Variation:

Draw circles on long piece of butcher paper for mural of heads.

Winger on Haircuts

Here's what I think about hair cuts. They can be good and they can be bad.

I like my hair now. It's pretty nice. I like how it ruffles when I shake my head. I do shake my head sometimes. Do you?

I did not like my last haircut. First the man accidentally poked my ear with those sharp scissors. Then I didn't like how short he cut my hair. I guess I should've told him; I need a little hair to keep my head warm. My nose got all tickly too, and stayed tickly, even when I'd wiped off all the hair. On the way home, I kept itching under my shirt. Do you ever get hair down your neck when you get a haircut?

Do you have your hair cut? Who cuts it?

Holistic Health Worker

Note:
Exercises in this section can be adapted for work in the health, healing, personal training, holistic counseling fields.

Stretches

Lead the children in simple stretching exercises. I have given "right" and "left" side directions, but you can adapt these for *young* early learners, simply by saying "one side, then the other."

While standing:
Reach as high as you can.
Slowly bend over and touch your toes, then slower still, straighten up again.
Move both hands from your waist to as far beyond your left ear as you can reach, as if a rocket ship is zooming out of your tummy up to the stars.
Change directions, with the rocket whooshing to your right.

While sitting cross-legged:
Put your hands on the ground behind you and tilt your head backwards, looking up.
Lean to the left, arching your right arm over your head like a rainbow.

continued

Stretches
(continued)

Switch directions, arching to your right with your left arm making the rainbow.

Bend forward, making your fingers crawl on the floor, like little spiders, as far as they can, straight ahead.

While lying on your backs:

Point your left toe. Bring your left foot straight up, as if your toes can reach to the sky. Slowly lower your leg to the floor.

Alternate with your right toe and leg.

Bring both feet up together.

Stretch your arms out on the floor, reaching as far away from your body as you can.

Stretch both your arms and legs out to the sides.

Variation: stretch to music, trying out different rhythms from time to time.

Healthy Eating

If possible, take your children with you to a grocery store that carries a variety of fresh produce. Better yet, take them to a farmer who sells fruits and vegetables right out of the field. Let the children choose their favorite fruits and vegetables. Let them purchase something new and unusual too.

Involve the children in snack preparation.

Healthy Bread & Sprouts

Include the children in baking your favorite whole grain bread. As you'll see, this is a several-hour project, suitable for making in the morning and eating for afternoon snack. If you don't have a recipe, here's one you might try:

Mmmm Good Bread

Soften 2 pkgs. yeast in 1/3 C. warm water.

Combine the following items in a large bowl:

3/4 C. oatmeal

1/4 C. rolled rye flakes (or use 1 C. oatmeal)

2 Tbsp. soy flour (optional)

1 Tbsp. nutritional yeast (optional)

1/4 C. milk powder (optional)

1 1/2 tsp. sea salt

3 Tbsp. olive or other good vegetable oil

1 C. bran

 Remove the bowl from the children and, at a *distance from them,* pour in 3 C. near-boiling water. Quickly stir. Let cool till just warm. Sing two favorite songs with the children while you wait.

Add the softened yeast and 3/4 C. molasses.

Stir in 3 1/2 C. whole wheat flour.

Add white flour, until the dough is no longer sticky (about 3 to 3 1/2 C.). You may have to do the final stirring as the dough will be heavy.

Turn out on a floured surface. Let the children knead the dough.

Put all the dough back together and place it in a bowl that you have rubbed with good vegetable oil. Turn the dough so the oiled surface is up. Cover. Let rise in a warm spot.

Punch down. Shape into 2 loaves. Place in oiled bread pans. Let rise 3/4 to 1 hour.

Bake at 350 degrees for 50 to 55 minutes. Be sure *an adult* puts the bread pans in and out of the oven. If your oven bakes hot, you may want to cover with foil for the last 15 minutes. The soy and milk powder will make the bread brown more quickly. Cool.

Slice and eat for snack with alfalfa sprouts and milk or juice.

For vegans (people who eat no animal products) or children with allergies, simply eliminate the milk powder and replace the flours with tolerant types.

Winger on Laughing

Laughter, chuckles, and giggles are really good for your health.

Play a laughing game with me. Here are the two rules:

1. We can say anything funny as long as it's not about another person.
2. We can't say stuff that's gross.

Ok, ready? Think of the silliest thing you can imagine. How about

a fish with an umbrella
or a grizzly bear with pink bows in her hair
or streets on stilts
or turtles on a trampoline.
Remember the two rules for this game?
_____ and _____

Now you think up something to make us laugh. _____

Activity

Soothing Sand Drawing

Put clean sand on a tray or in a flat container (something like a cat litter box works great).
Allow the children to draw in the sand, one or two at a time.

Guided Group Meditation

Choose a time when the children will be able to get calm, not for instance right after a sweet dessert.

Have the children lie down in a warm and comfortable spot, on a rug, on sleeping mats, or even outdoors on blankets in nice weather.

Use this or your own guided meditation to help children be able to access inner peace:

Take a deep breath. Now take another deep breath. It's OK to close your eyes. I will make sure that no one bothers you while we are meditating.

Take one more deep breath.

In your mind imagine that you're in a very safe and restful place.

Now imagine yourself sitting on a little beach alongside a stream.

Imagine that you smell the fresh water on mossy rocks.

Imagine that you hear birds singing.

Imagine that you see a chipmunk running out on a branch that hangs over the creek.

In turn, give children a chance to lead this simple meditation while the others remain lying down. Usher the leader through describing where they might be, what they might smell, hear, and see. Depending on your group's listening abilities, you may have to give turns to include the whole group over a period of several days.

Whole Body Walking

Establish a course, either around your play yard or gym, or on a small track in a neighborhood park. If you can, make the course circle round, so that you can do laps with the children.

Demonstrate walking, swinging your arms in rhythm.

Tell the children that simple walking will give their bodies, minds, and spirits a refreshing workout.

Walk round the course with your children, one, two, three times a day. If possible, include this as a regular part of every day.

Quiet Spot (if you don't already have one)

For some sensitive children, preschools and child care centers can be overwhelming, simply because of the number of people with whom they must interact. Talk with your children, letting them assess with you: Would they like a quiet spot? Do they *need* a quiet spot?

Beforehand, think of two or three possible areas in your physical space that you might feel comfortable altering. Let the children help you choose which would be best. Maybe you could make a pillowed corner indoors. Or perhaps you could designate a quiet spot in your play yard, under a tree or in an area where you could add comfortable benches (even smooth logs to sit on). Be clear what will work, safety-wise and logistically, in your setting. Encouraging quiet, reflective, calming times in this stress-filled world can build a habit that will serve them for life.

Of course, this project will totally depend on your facility. Any quiet spot must be situated so you can see and hear your children at all times.

What Are We?

Some children, even at three and four, seem to be tuned in to another dimension. I'm thinking, for instance, of the four-year-old boy who wanted to, and did, draw a series of pictures of the dozen different daffodils I brought in, each picture unique, each whimsically executed. While most of the group saw a row of yellow and white flowers, he noted their differences and responded, with fascination. He was the kind of child who would initiate conversations about what we are.

For these few children, you might simply mention "Spirit" as *the part within us* that knows who we are and why we're here on earth, the part of us that connects to all other living things.

The child might make a picture that shows what she thinks of as her own Spirit, using favorite painting or drawing materials.

Once again, you will be the one to determine if this activity is appropriate for any of your children. Some parents prefer to handle any discussion of "Spirit" themselves.

Homemaker

Homemaking

Sometimes, even just from steady use, our preschool and child care center "home corners" become a mishmash of tools and supplies that bear little resemblance to the actual job of managing a home. We can improve on our home corners. Consider pretend equipment for:

cleaning	child care
decorating	pet and plant care
meal planning	yard work
meal preparation	car maintenance
shopping	servicing appliances
clothing maintenance	running errands
washing	taxi service
folding	paying bills
ironing	recycling/garbage take-out

Skippety on Homemaking

Even if one person
stays at home,
it takes more than one
to keep house.

Even when kids
go to school all day long,
they need to help
more than a mouse.

Somehow the dishes
must get washed.
Somehow the clothes
cleaned too.

Somehow somebody
needs to fix dinner.
It might be a
casserole, or stew.

Somebody has to
bring home the groceries.
Then they'll need
putting away.

Somebody needs to pick up
the living room.
Sometimes it takes
all day!

When everyone shares
in the housework,
it makes a home
feel good.

Housework shouldn't
be done by one person,
even if
one person could.

Job Chart

Does your home corner have a chart in it, with a way to sign up for taking turns on at least some of the jobs below?

Add stick-on cards with children's names, or make a chart on a chalkboard.

Job Chart—Caring for the parts of our home corner

S   M   T   W   Th   F   S

washing dishes
sweeping floors
preparing food
sorting and taking out the garbage and recycling
cleaning and folding clothes

Unanticipated Appreciation for Homemakers (one idea)

Fold a large sheet of construction paper.

Cut a large construction paper card in the shape of a house, with the fold along the left side.
Show children how to draw and cut out hearts on a fold.

Offer a variety of materials for the hearts:
cloth
colored paper
newspaper
even sandpaper

Let children adorn their houses with hearts of their own choosing.

Variation: Offer crayons for pictures and the printed words "Thank you" to be cut out and pasted onto the card. Or, let the children come up with their own way to show appreciation for the homemakers in their families.

Weaver Finch on Homemaking

Come gather round and I'll tell you a story.

Once there were two families who lived side by side. The kids were cousins. One family had a mother and two children. The mother worked all day at a job and the children went to school. The other family had a mother, a father, and one child. The mother and father both worked at jobs all day too, and their son went to a child care center.

Both households had a problem. There was very little time for homemaking. One day the cousins were playing in the side yard and the parents were out front talking. They were talking about their problem.

The mothers and father hadn't realized that there were some kinds of housework each of them liked, and some kinds of housework each of them didn't like. So they decided to try to help each other.

I need three children to act this out. (As you tell the story, assign children to the parts.)

One mother liked fixing things, the father liked cooking, and the other mother liked shopping.

I need three more children to act in this play.

The children thought that they didn't like any housework, until the father asked for help cooking. He got a volunteer right away. One mother asked for help fixing things and one mother wanted help with the shopping. Now there was work that each of the children really needed to do. And because the adult they worked with liked the job at hand, the children found it was fun too.

Then came the not-so-fun jobs. What's left in taking care of a home? (Brainstorm list: dishes, vacuuming, dusting, laundry, cleaning bathroom, lawn mowing, etc. It's best to allow an incomplete list that comes from the children's own awareness. There's no need to try to drill in all the various aspects of keeping up a home.)

(to the group) You know a lot about homemaking!

Weaver Finch on Homemaking
(continued)

The families in our story divided all the not-so-fun jobs. Every week they traded around those not-so-fun jobs, so nobody got really tired or frustrated.

At the end of their first month of helping with homemaking, what do you suppose the two families decided to do? _____ Actually, (you're right) they enjoyed their jobs now that they were helping each other. Doing all their housework in teams, made the housework fun.

Finch, three, two, one. This story is done.

House Painter

Project

House Painting Mural

Pass out paper triangles, squares, and rectangles.

Roll out a length of paper long enough to accommodate a spot for each child.

Let the children combine the shapes to make their own houses, which they glue onto the mural.

Using poster paints, the children can paint their houses.

Imaginative Play

House Painting Outdoors

brushes
rollers
paint tray
big wheel or trike
wagon
buckets
water

Painted Cottages

graham crackers for the cottages
"paint" made of cream cheese and blueberries, oranges, or straw-berries

Using plastic knives, the children can "paint" their own graham cracker cottages.

Add available edibles for windows (pumpkin seeds, for instance).
 If you have an adult helper, it would be pretty easy for him to cut jicama into small rectangles for every child to have a door for their cottage. If you haven't tried jicama, you're in for a treat. Buy jicama fresh in the vegetable department of any large grocery store. It has a sweet, fresh taste and a crisp texture, softer than carrots, a little harder than apples.

House Painting Indoors

large appliance boxes
poster paints
Have the children help you draw windows, doors, trim, down-spouts or whatever they want, to transform the boxes into houses.
Let the children each paint a section.

Weaver Finch on House Painting

Come gather round and I'll tell you a story.

Once there was a town where all the people loved colors. They loved color so much that they had a special holiday four times a year. The townspeople cooked all kinds of fancy food and the house painters painted all day. At night, they celebrated in the town square.

One spring the house painters painted the whole town _____.

Then that summer they changed all the two-story buildings to _____.

continued

Weaver Finch on House Painting
(continued)

The grocer's family went on a long vacation. They saw golden wheat blowing in the wind. Besides which they grew especially partial to the fields of spotted cows. When they got back, the grocer talked to the town painters, and that fall the painters made spots of _____ and _____ on all the wheat-colored houses.

Then came winter, with the cold and snow. To warm up the town, the house painters painted everything _____.

House painting continued as a tradition that was passed on in the town from grandpas and grandmas, aunts and uncles, to their children and their children's children. Four times a year the whole town celebrated a new color. Four times a year they enjoyed a change.

Finch, three, two, one. This story is done.

Skippety on House Painting

I built a house in town.
But the neighbors all around
said, "Oo oo oo!
Please don't paint it blue!"
"Oh dear," they said, "oh dread."
"You wouldn't paint it red!"

I wouldn't paint it beige or gold
I wanted my house bright and bold.
Not all the pale colors I'd seen.
I wanted my house purple and green.
So here's what I had to do.
I moved my house. Wouldn't you?

My house is now up on a hill,
My house happily stands there still.
It's tucked behind a grove of trees,
the only "oooo's" come from the breeze.
I painted my house green and purple,
With a stripe of yellow around the middle.

Inventor

Inventor's Workshop

Fill a gadget supply box with *safe* odds and ends.(Ask parents to contribute from their "junk drawers.")

Designate a table or an area with a sign: Inventor's Workshop.

Explain to your children that an inventor makes things. Talk about items used in everyday life that someone invented. Talk about how inventors earn money by selling their ideas to companies and marketing their products through national conventions such as the International Housewares Show.

Two at a time, let children take turns inventing gadgets. Ask "What would your gadget do?"

The children will use their imaginations, communicate with their partner and helping adult, and work with their hands using a variety of materials. There is no expectation that the inventions will actually work.

Project

Creative Movement

I'm a Machine

Stand with children in a circle.

Leader begins: "I'm a machine that goes up and down."

Everybody repeats, acting out: "I'm a machine that goes up and down."

Continue with machine:

that spins

that makes a lot of noise

that has wheels

that clicks

that freezes

that rings

Use children's suggestions. If your group is accustomed to working in pairs, you might have one child act the part of the machine, the other child pretend to use it.

Snack

Invent a Salad

Set out bowls of chopped lettuce, cabbage (purple and green), cucumbers, oranges, apples, parsley, celery, and raisins.

Children dish up their own combination of ingredients.

Snack

Invent a Roll

Using prepared biscuit dough, let each child shape the biscuit round into a roll.

Let children smell bottles of cinnamon sugar, jam, sugar and nutmeg mix, and honey butter. Each child will dip their dough into a dab of their favorite topping.

Bake on greased cookie sheets at 400 degrees, for 9 to 10 minutes.

 Be sure *an adult* puts the cookie sheets in and out of the oven. Cool.

What Can you Make with a Paper Bag?

Set out a stack of paper bags, glue, scissors, and paints.

By ripping, cutting, gluing, and painting, children create. Give no directions towards a specific product. Challenge the children to invent something new.

Inventing a Language

Sketch the following motions onto separate 5″ × 7″ cards. Stick-figure sketches will do. Or enlist the help of an artistic parent or volunteer. You can also print the words clearly below the pictures as a prereading piece.

clap hands	wave hands
stamp feet	clap behind back
pat head	turn around
sit down	wiggle hips
rub tummy	clap hands under one leg
hop	jump up and down

Put the cards in a paper bag.

Stand with the children in a circle.

Let the child to your left draw a card. The child then holds up the card, so that everyone can see it. Help the child read the card, if need be. Then the child sets the card down at his feet, face up.

The child leads everyone (in place) in acting out the card.

Then move to the next child on the left, repeating showing the card, reading, and acting it out.

Inventing variation: After going through all the body motions, divide into pairs. Let the children use this body language to "speak" to each other. See if they can interpret the body language into words. What is their partner telling them?

Weaver Finch on Inventing

Come gather round and I'll tell you a story.

Once there was an eighteen-year-old girl who lived in a little house at the bend in a river. The girl's name was Melinda. Melinda cared about her family. She rarely visited them though.
Melinda just liked staying home. She also liked tinkering.

Melinda had built a magnificent workshop next to her house. Most days, if you wanted to talk to Melinda, that's where you'd find her, tinkering in her workshop.

Even though Melinda rarely left her comfy spot by the river, and her trips away were usually made just to buy more materials for her projects, Melinda thought about her family every day. She took great pleasure in inventing gadgets to make their lives better.

For instance, Melinda's father used a wheelchair to get around, just like I do. For years he'd lived in an old-fashioned town that had high curbs on the sidewalks with no wheelchair ramps. Melinda made a lift that would hoist his wheelchair down and up whenever he crossed the street. Even after the town workers put in slopes on the sidewalks, Melinda's father used the hoist to get up the front steps when he went into houses that didn't have ramps.

Melinda also thought up gizmos for her sister who was a chef. She made a machine that flipped pan-size pancakes. She also made long-handled grabbers that could lift spaghetti out of a pot.

Melinda liked inventing things for all her family. Sometimes her gadgets and gizmos were so unusual and so useful, she would apply for a patent. If the government granted her a patent it meant she was the first person ever to think up and make that new invention. Then Melinda would sell the idea to a company that would make lots of whatever she had invented. That's how Melinda earned money for living.

Weaver Finch on Inventing
(continued)

Melinda was happy in her work. When she wasn't drawing designs, or sawing or welding or working on fitting pieces together, she was relaxing by the river. Melinda had a fondness for the Black-Capped Chickadees who landed in the huckleberry bushes by the riverbank. Ha ha! You guessed it. Melinda couldn't help inventing things for the birds too. What do you suppose she made for them? _____ How about you draw some pictures of the inventions Melinda made for her bird friends.

Finch, three, two, one. This story is done.

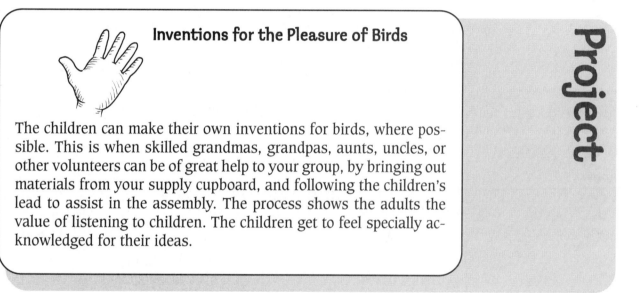

Inventions for the Pleasure of Birds

The children can make their own inventions for birds, where possible. This is when skilled grandmas, grandpas, aunts, uncles, or other volunteers can be of great help to your group, by bringing out materials from your supply cupboard, and following the children's lead to assist in the assembly. The process shows the adults the value of listening to children. The children get to feel specially acknowledged for their ideas.

Project

Laboratory
Scientist

Mixtures

Ask parents to look through their spice racks for long-past-fresh herbs and spices. Would they like to donate to science?

Set up experiment trays with:

spices in separate containers   plastic measuring cups
pitcher of water   vinegar
small funnel   stirring spoons
plastic bottles   measuring spoons

 Let the children enjoy mixing. You may need to set a limit of the amount of spices allowed for each in order to make the supplies last for everyone. A volunteer can help divvy out the supplies.

Freeze/Melt

Let children mix several sets of ingredients in small plastic containers. Possible ingredients:

paper, which the children shred, and water

dirt and water

plastic bits (like pieces of straws or bottle caps) and water

weeds, which the children chop, grind or mash, and water

Children can freeze the mixtures,

examine,

let melt,

and examine again.

Record their findings on an observation sheet, using symbols (such as a picture of an ice cube) along with words.

Experimental Cookies

Let groups of two or three children create their own cookies using the following possible ingredients. Before they begin, talk about how desserts can be too sweet or too salty. See if this helps them think through their choice of ingredients. Resist directing them though.

flour, in maximum of 2 cups

margarine, honey, peanut butter, in maximum of 1/2 cup each

coconut, oatmeal, in maximum of 3/4 cup each

mashed banana or 1 packet pudding mix

and vanilla, salt, baking powder, in maximum of a tsp. each

Note the advantage to replacing egg with pudding mix or mashed banana: the children will undoubtedly want to sample their dough, and mustn't if raw eggs are involved.

Let children spoon dough onto greased cookie sheets, and bake for 10 minutes at 350 degrees. Be sure *an adult* puts the cookie sheets in and out of the oven. Let cool.

Remember to focus on the process rather than the product. The cookies will be edible, some tastier than others. The empowering experience is what matters.

Color Mixing

In a water table, offer:
plastic bottles of colored water
small pitcher
funnel
plastic tubing, if you have some, large enough to fit funnel into

Children can pour, watching colors mix and move.

Skippety on Mixing and Making

Sing ho!
Oh-merry-o.
I love mixing,
oh-derry-o.

Stir up my mix
and pour it out flat.
Sing ho-di-o-ho
oh merry-oh.

Pound it and squish
and pat-a-pat splat.
Sing ho-di-o-day.
oh merry-ay.

Mixing and pouring
is what I do best.
Sing ho-di-o-ho
oh-merry-oh.

Just give me ingredients,
I'll do the rest.
Sing ho-di-o-day,
oh merry-ay.

Sing ho (hold "ho" for several counts)
Oh-merry-o!
I love mixing,
oh-derry-o.

Winger on Mixing

Here's what I think about mixing: I love mixing things!

Oh wow! Did I get in trouble one time though. I was using the old spices my grandma brought me. When I went into the bathroom to get water, I saw this bottle that was a sunshiny yellow color. So I poured some in the spices. When I was mixing that up, my eyes started to burn. I cried and tears poured down my face. I got Mom right away, cuz my eyes hurt really bad.

Mom was sure mad! You see, we had an agreement that I would always ask her when I want to use something for mixing. She was scared that I'd burnt my eyes with the chemical smell. We went right to the hospital emergency room. That was scary enough. The doctor who looked at me said I was lucky I hadn't ruined my eyes. A nurse put in some eye drops, and about three days later my eyes didn't hurt anymore.

I sure learned a lesson. Now, I *always* check out my ingredients with an adult before I do my mixing! I want you to too.

Librarian

Library

shelves, made out of cardboard bricks or wooden blocks
books
slips of paper for check-out cards
cart, or toy flatbed truck, for reshelving
stamp, for stamping check-out cards
check-out desk or table
research books, such as encyclopedias, atlas, dictionary
recipe-type file box
computer made out of a cardboard box, with paper screen and a knob made of plastic lid (attached with a brad through a hole in lid)
keyboard, made out of large shoe box lid, covered, with keys (the letters, numbers, and symbols) drawn on
a wire connecting the computer boxes

Skippety on Being a Librarian

If I was a librarian

I think that I would see

you and you and you

at the library.

Books

stone ground wheat crackers
Have the children spread cream cheese along left edge of cracker.
Lay a thin slice of deli chicken, or meat substitute, cut in cracker-size squares on top.
Add more "pages" and top "cover" with cream cheese "binding."

Snacks

Cataloging

Let the children sort and categorize all books in your library.
Put a book with illustrated cover, or a sign, in front of each area, such as animals, people, projects, study books, etc.

Activity

Make a Book

Make books to add to your library:

Let children cut out old magazine pictures and glue these into their books, with topics that fit into the categories in their library. For the younger children, instead of reading books, these can be "looking books."

Depending on the children's ages, and interests, you could also write down children's dictated words. Then adults can read these books back to the children when theirs are checked out at the pretend library.

Winger on Libraries

Here's what I think about libraries: Wow! All those books and tapes! I love them.

Sometimes the people in the pictures look like they're having so much fun, I want to be in the book with them. When the story's really good, I feel like I'm right there with the characters. And when the stories are funny, I can't stop laughing.

When I walk into the library, I feel like I'm visiting my friends, old friends in stories I know almost by heart, and new friends in books we haven't read yet. Sometimes it's really hard to choose a book. I want to read them all.

How do you feel about libraries?

Weaver Finch on Libraries

Come gather round and I'll tell you a story.

Once, in a time very different from now, only the adult sections of the libraries got used. The children's libraries were empty most of the time. Children were either at computer school, or in front of their home TV/video systems.

When the computerized schools began, teachers no longer read to the children or helped them check out books. And the parents got tired of trying to get their children away from the entertainment centers long enough to read. Anyway, it was easier and quieter for the adults, with all the children sitting in front of their computer screens. I'm happy to tell you though, that there was one dear children's librarian who kept doing her job. She kept buying books, hoping someday that the children would return.

One day, the lights went out all over the city. There was a huge power failure. So many people had turned on their computers and video game centers, that the city blew out all the transformers, from downtown way out to the country. The computer schools closed and none of the home entertainment systems worked for a week.

The first couple days the children just wandered from house to house. They'd forgotten how to play games or how to ride bikes. They'd forgotten just about everything. Then one day a young boy noticed the library doors were open, but the boy was afraid to go in by himself. He called down the street to his friends. Together they went into the library.

Actually the children were so young that they'd never been in a library before. They couldn't believe all the rows of books. When one girl happened into the children's section, she quickly called to all her friends. That children's librarian I was telling you about was right there, asking questions about their interests. Since most of them had no special interests, the librarian took them through the shelves, pointing out the different sections. "We have books on hobbies, books on animals from our area, and other books on animals from all over the world. We have books with stories about children like you, and books about faraway times with dragons and castles and horses galloping across the countryside." The children had learned how to read at computer school, but they'd never read stories in books. How do you think they felt looking at all those books? ＿＿＿＿

continued

Weaver Finch on Libraries
(continued)

That night when the parents called their children to come for supper, there was no response. Do you know where they were? The children were still in the library, on the steps of the library, on the stone wall outside the library, reading and looking at books. And the dear children's librarian? Her jaws hurt from smiling so much.

Finch, three, two, one. This story is done.

Mechanic

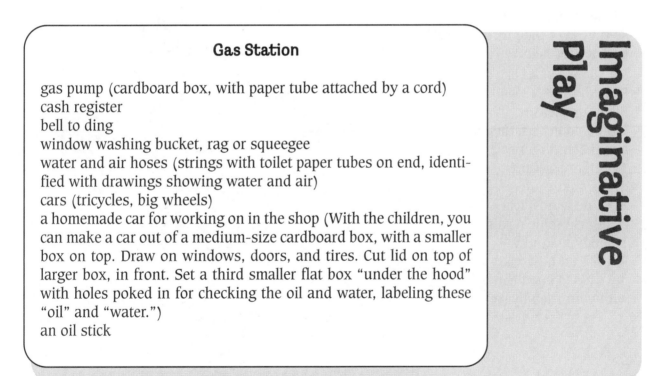

Gas Station

gas pump (cardboard box, with paper tube attached by a cord)
cash register
bell to ding
window washing bucket, rag or squeegee
water and air hoses (strings with toilet paper tubes on end, identified with drawings showing water and air)
cars (tricycles, big wheels)
a homemade car for working on in the shop (With the children, you
can make a car out of a medium-size cardboard box, with a smaller
box on top. Draw on windows, doors, and tires. Cut lid on top of
larger box, in front. Set a third smaller flat box "under the hood"
with holes poked in for checking the oil and water, labeling these
"oil" and "water.")
an oil stick

Snack

Mechanic's Snack

Nuts and bolts:
pretzel sticks and raisins
Mechanic's Shake:
Warm 1 cup milk per child.
Add 1 Tbsp. creamy peanut butter and 1 tsp. molasses per serving.
Blend with a wire whisk.

Skippety on Mechanics

(Some people don't like working in grease,
so they take their cars to service stations or
garages for help.)

Ding ding!
Fill'er up please.
Would you check the oil
and the antifreeze?
The right back tire
needs a little air.
And the windshield wiper
could use some repair.
Thank you kindly.
I never get nervous;
my car's in good hands
with your friendly service.

Weaver Finch on Mechanics

Come gather round and I'll tell you a story.

I used to think I couldn't work on a car. I used to think that was men's work. Then years ago my daughter gave me this wonderful repair manual. I found out I could change the oil and even give my car a tune-up. I kept my own cars running good for years.

Once, before I got my wheelchair, I remember it was the middle of winter. We lived in a little country house at the end of a long lane lined with blackberries. We didn't have a garage, so if I worked on my car, I had to work outside in the driveway. If I took the car to a mechanic to be fixed, I'd have to wait in the shop. I wasn't very good at waiting, so I chose to fix the car myself.

Our car had been spitting and sputtering for days. A friend at a car parts store told me I'd be needing a water pump. So I picked one up, but I had so many other things to do, I didn't get to fixing the car that day, or the next. Before I knew it, my car wouldn't run at all. When I tried to start it, I heard water pouring out underneath the car. I went straight for my toolbox.

It'd been snowing. I slid on my back underneath the car. In some places there was freezing cold snow, in other places mud where the water had overflowed. I couldn't move much under the car, just a little from side to side. I still remember how my hands felt. They got burning cold within minutes, even though I had gloves on.

I located the water pump. With my crescent wrench, I tried to loosen the bolts, but there wasn't enough room to get a tight hold. So I slithered out and got my socket wrench with a long-handled extension. I scooted back under the car, fitted the wrench up over my head and started to turn. Splat. A big chunk of muddy snow landed in my face. I tried to wipe it off with my sleeve, but my elbow got stuck on a pipe. I had to roll sideways so I could move my arm to keep working.

continued

Weaver Finch on Mechanics
(continued)

When I got the socket wrench positioned again, I tugged and tugged and grunted and even banged a little. Finally the nut gave way. I had to do that four times. And three of those times I dropped the nut. My fingers were numb from searching around in the snow. The water pump came off though, but it almost landed on my face. Of course water came out with it, which poured onto my coat and dribbled down my neck.

With my foot, I snagged the new water pump, which was lying by the side of the car. I scooted it up where I could reach it with my hand. By then my teeth were chattering and my shoulders shaking. But I got the new pump to fit up onto the bolts, with the gasket sealed underneath. Then I searched around, trying to find where I'd set the socket wrench. It was under my left side, so I pulled it out from under me and tightened down the nuts. I was so cold, I could barely get out from under the car. My stocking hat came off, so my hair was full of muddy snow.

Shivering and even moaning a little, I got into the car. I turned the key, and vroom, room, room, the engine started. "Good for me!" I thought as I turned off the engine and hobbled into the house for a nice hot shower.

Finch, three, two, one. This story is done.

Naturalist

Bird Feeder

A simple bird feeder can be made with the children. All you need is a board, about 1′ × 3′, and some 1″ × 1‴'s.

Saw the smaller pieces in strips to match the lengths and widths of your board. *(If you do the sawing near children, use a hand saw rather than an electric saw, for safety, and still have the children stand at a distance from the saw.)* Remember that if you put the strips lengthwise first, the width strips will be 2″ shorter than the actual width. Measure the precise width before you saw the final strips.

Let the children nail the 1″ × 1‴'s around the edge of the board. Screw four eye hooks into the corners. Once you get the eye screw started, then stick a narrow screwdriver in the eye, the children can turn the screwdriver to finish the job.

Hang the feeder, attaching a thin nylon rope to the eyes. Be sure the feeder's not accessible to cats or other predators.

Let the children take turns filling the feeder with wild birdseed.

With the Birds

hulled sunflower seeds
sesame seeds
nutmeats
berries
While this is food suitable for birds, the children will enjoy the snack items themselves. If eaten outdoors, any seeds that fall to the ground will most likely be eaten later by the birds.

Erosion

If you have an outdoor area that can be allotted to dirt and water play for a time, allow the children to experiment with building mounds, pouring water over them, watching channels form, creating diversions for the water.

The children will need warm weather and parent or guardians' knowledge so they can bring appropriate play clothes.

If your area permits, follow up informally, while you're out on a walk in nature, by observing actual erosion. Also look for areas that are not eroding. Talk just a bit about how vegetation prevents erosion.

Observing Nature

Use a plastic container such as a cat litter tray, or a lined box. Fill with dirt and small growing things from your locale. Try to disturb just a very small area, being careful to take only plants that exist in abundance. Smooth over your digging site.

Let the children lightly wet the dirt every few days with a watering can, as if it were raining.

Over a several week period:

Watch for sprouting plants and new buds.

Talk about the animals that would live in such areas.

Let the children decorate the sides of the box with cut-outs or pictures of those animals.

Let the children color and cut out construction-paper birds.

Glue these and pictures of any flying insects they might want to add onto thin sticks, which they place into the dirt.

You have replicated a mini-ecosystem.

Let the children help you return the items and dirt to the outdoors when done.

Touch and Smell

If possible, take your group on a woods walk. If not, gather the following yourself:

aromatic dried bits of cedar bough or what-have-you locally
(cedar) bark (only use what's already fallen from trees)
(cedar) wood
humus-type dirt
moss
dry leaves

Divide your collected bits into two sets, with half of each of your items in each set.

Put a piece of each item in a separate sniffing jar. (Make sniffing jars by covering a small container so the contents are hidden. Either poke holes in the lid or put mesh over the top.)

Put the other half into small paper bags, one type in each.

Let the children take turns trying to identify the items by touch and smell.

Project

Land Management

Cut off the top half of large paper bags.

Cut out three or four peek holes in one side, about two inches from the bottom.

Let children make their own parks, with items found on walks:

sticks

dried moss

leaves

fallen seed pods *(Make sure children don't put these in their mouths.)*

Display at child height, so they are able to peek into the created woods environments.

Skippety on Beaver and Fungus

Beaver and fungus
and bugs among us,
polliwogs, jumping frogs,
fallen logs, berry bogs,
great blue heron,
mackerel,
salt grass sand,
forgotten pool.
Old stands of trees
wave in the breeze,
with skittering squirrels and 'munks
all up and down the trunks,
hovering birds in the air,
glistening spiders on their web . . .
Web?

We're a part of that web of life.
If we maintain the balance
we can give up the strife (over). . . .
(Repeat, ending with:
We can give up the strife.)

Weaver Finch on Working with a Naturalist

Come gather round and I'll tell you a story.

When I was a young woman, I got to work with a naturalist one summer. I was helping her research the many kinds of plants and animals that lived in our neck of the woods.

That was one of the best jobs I've ever had. I'd get up early in the morning and drive this old green pickup truck way up in the hills. I'd park the truck at a trail head, and load my notebooks, my plant and animal identification books, my binoculars, my lunch, and two big water bottles into my pack. Then I'd walk four miles on the trail until I got to the meadow we were studying. I liked that trail. It went up and down through the woods and past open spaces where I could see out across the valley.

The naturalist had lots of other things to do, so I often went by myself. Some of my time I spent writing down what kinds of plants I found in the meadow. I'd count how many of each plant I saw and write that on the meadow map. I'd also sit on the ground, leaned up against a tree, and just watch. That was part of my job! If I was quiet, the animals wouldn't realize I was there, or if they did, they weren't afraid of me. I saw a silver fox come out of the woods, and several black-tailed deer. I'd write down what I saw in my notebook. I often stayed into the early evening when the animals would come to drink at the creek.

Sometimes the naturalist and I would camp all night at the edge of the meadow. That's when we saw the skunk and a family of raccoons. Coyotes came through too. And in the early morning, elk.

Even to this day I can remember the smell of that meadow. The sun on the wildflowers . . . well, it's not like anything I've smelled since. It had a thick smell. Wild and sweet, mixed with the smell of warmed rocks. A really good mountain meadow smell.

Finch, three, two, one. This story is done.

Pilot

Imaginative Play

Piloting a Plane

large, refrigerator-size box for the fuselage

Cut short wings out of another piece of cardboard.
Poke sets of holes in the fuselage and the wide end of the wings.
Fold down about four inches on the wide side of the wings.
Fasten the wings onto the fuselage with short lengths of cord.
Cut a door for getting into the cockpit. Cut out windows.

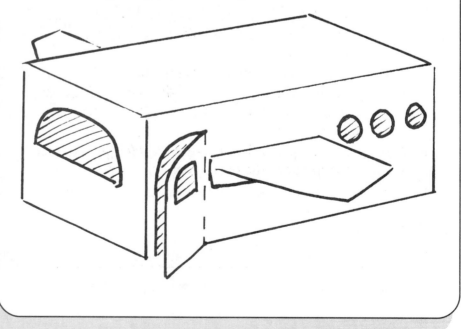

Piloting a Plane
(continued)

Put in two small chairs for pilot and co-pilot.

Make an instrument panel out of any set of dials and knobs. (Lids with brads holding them to a piece of cardboard will do, if you don't have recycled dials from an old appliance on hand.)

flight log (small notebook) and pen
flashlights for directing on runway

Airplane

Remove the bottom of an empty, washed tuna, water chestnut can (or equivalent).

Flatten it slightly to use as oblong cutter.

Have the snack helpers:

Roll out sugar cookie or biscuit dough.

Cut two oblongs for each airplane.

Put one on top of the other, sticking with a dab of water.

Stick half a date on the tail, pinching to make a back rudder.

 An adult can cut the other half date into a square, then cut in all around outside, making it look like a propeller blade.

Affix it with a dab of water onto nose of the plane. (If this propeller design is too time-consuming, affix a round peppermint candy, the kind with color radiating out, to the nose of the airplane.)

Bake as per recipe. Be sure *an adult* puts the pans in and out of the oven. Cool.

Parachutes

cupcake papers, doubled so they don't rip
lengths of embroidery thread
small pine cones for baskets
rubber bands

Put rubber bands tightly around the pine cones.

Children can attach the pine cones by looping embroidery thread under the rubber band and taping both ends, with small pieces of masking tape, to the outside of the cupcake papers. The parachutes won't look as tidy this way, but when doubled, the papers will stay together only if taped on the outside.

Find a safe place, such as the top of an outdoor climber, for the children to release their parachutes. Supervise, so there is an open landing area where the parachutes won't come down on the children.

Skippety on Flying

Tina and Tony
flew up in a plane.
They flew in the clouds.
They flew in the rain.
They flew straight up,
then down, down, down.
Tina landed the plane.
Tony taxied it round.

Skippety on Take-off

Buckle seat belts.
Turn the key on.
Rrhr, rhr, rhr.
Check the gauges,
wing flaps, rudder.
Rrhr, rhr, rhr.
Taxi round
to face the runway.
Rhh, buh, bump, rhrh.
Scan the sky
for other airplanes.
Rhr, rhr, rhr.
Pull the throttle.
Back the yoke out.
Slowly, rhrh, woah.
Steady, rhrh, woah.
Rhrhrh, whoah.
Rhrhrh, whoah.
Eeeee, eeeee! Prrrr.

Winger, More on Flying

I don't need an airplane to fly. But I can fly higher in an airplane than flying with just my wings. When I'm in an airplane, I see sky and sky and sky, everywhere. It's pretty good in an airplane. A little bumpy sometimes. Which is strange, since there's no road to bump on. It's only air up there. I like being right in the middle of the air.

It's weird. There're no streets in the air. I suppose you know that. No stop signs, or turn lights. And airplanes fly past each other, and over each other and under each other, just fine. Pilots use instruments on the dashboard of their airplanes to tell them when other planes are near. Not instruments like you play music on. But instruments like in a car, like gas gauges and stuff. The air controller who watches from the tower tells them if planes are close by when they're flying near an airport. Of course, if it's foggy or if it's nighttime, the controller uses instruments, too, to keep the planes safe.

Have you ever flown in an airplane?
What was it like?
Did you like it?
If you haven't ridden in an airplane, do you think you would like to go for a plane ride some day?

Police Officer

Note:

Focusing on the police profession may set off heated discussion. Or children may become withdrawn and unusually quiet. Try to listen to the heart behind the children's words. What has been their experience? What has caused a child to feel either positively or negatively towards police?

Police are often involved after accidents or emergencies. Does play acting "police" remind the child of a scary or sad experience? By watching and listening to the play, you may be able to ask just the right question at some later time, for the child to share his feelings.

Visit with the Police

While some children will think of the police as helpers, even heroes, others may have had negative contact with the police, due to family or neighborhood situations. Invite in police officers, men and women, to personalize the profession. It can be a great comfort to children to hear a police officer say, "Call if you ever need help."

Activity

Activity

Staying Fit

Police exercise to stay in shape. Set up a police training center to do:
stretches
sit-ups
jumping jacks
running in place
Set up an obstacle course in your gym or outdoors. (Cardboard boxes work really well for running between, over, and around.)

Imaginative Play

Police Station

If at all possible, take your children to a police station. Ask that the children be allowed to sit in a police car. Ask what the police men and women do at work. The children will naturally expand their play after talking with real officers in a police station setting.
clipboard/pen
report paper
flashlight
a map of your area
a pad for writing tickets
a badge
walkie talkies (recycled check boxes from a bank)
a modified first aid kit suitable for play (with small bandages, an ace bandage, a splint made simply out of a triangle of cardboard, and a dish towel sling, for instance)

Police do many other things besides using their weapons. Pretend gun play cannot be allowed in early childhood settings. Talk with your children about other police activities that they can play, such as rescue, calming disputes, traffic safety, talking to schools about saying no to gang activity and drugs, helping younger children get involved in positive activities like neighborhood sports.

Search Drills

Police have to be observant, able to get from one place to another safely, but in a hurry. Give children direction cards with clues of what to look for, in an extended search activity.

For instance, if you have an outdoor play yard, you might use a series of numbered cards such as this, placed for pretend play, to retrieve missing property:

1. Picture of a police car going to a cone (with the word *drive* and an arrow pointing across the pavement to a traffic cone). Children can easily pretend big wheels or trikes are police cars.
2. Picture of a tree. ("Go to the tree.")
3. At the back base of the tree, a picture of a box beside a building. (Go to the nearest building and look for a box.)
4. The missing item, such as a stuffed animal, will be in the box.

You can make the search course as involved as you like, either with a series of cards or on a map drawn to fit your play area. With your help, children can make search courses for each other.

Winger on Police

Here's what I feel about police: a little nervous, a little happy.

This is why: Last year my older brother graduated from a special school. He got a job as a police officer. Well, I think it's scary for my brother to be out there, you know, like when people are shooting guns and the police have to stop them. I don't want my brother to get hurt.

But everybody in our family says they're really proud of my brother. He always wanted to be a police officer. And he studied really hard in school. My brother knows all the stuff to help people and to keep himself safe. Even though it's dangerous, I'm glad he gets to do what he's always wanted to do. I know he'll be a good police officer. He really cares about people.

Finger Prints

Mix fairly thin black poster paint.
Let children stir it with their fingers.
Blot fingers on paper towels if need be.
Make finger prints, on smooth white or light-colored paper.
Label the prints. Compare. Do they look the same?

Weaver Finch on Police

Come gather round and I'll tell you a story.

One time, not very long ago, I was by myself in a city. I was pretty near exhausted, looking around, trying to tell by the street signs which would be the shortest way back to where I was staying. So I wasn't really paying attention. All of a sudden a man ran up to me. He bumped right into my wheelchair. As I was trying to steady myself, he yanked my purse away from me.

Another man on the street saw what happened and tried to grab the thief, but the thief pushed him down. I started yelling, "Help! Police!"

As it turned out, there was a policeman in a car at the very next corner. He saw me, but he was going in the opposite direction from the thief, so he called on the radio to another officer who was on foot just down the street. That second policewoman was ready. As the thief ran by, she grabbed his arm, spun him around and had his hands pinned behind his back in just a couple of seconds. The thief had to get in the police car, and I got my purse back. I was grateful for the police officer's help.

Have the police ever helped you?

Finch, three, two, one. This story is done.

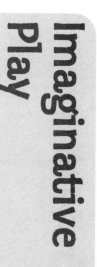

Postal Worker

Imaginative Play

Postal Delivery

With the children, set up two houses (tables, boxes, or whatever), a post office, and two more businesses. (Signs can identify the post office and businesses, as per children's designs.)

Supplies: recycled envelopes, scratch paper

If you set up the idea of letter delivery, the following, or some variation of this imaginative play, could take place:

Some children pretend to be living in their houses. They write letters and set them out in their mailbox, as if being mailed.

A mail carrier arrives on big wheels or on foot, depending on whether the play is indoors or out. The carrier puts the letters in a letter bag. (Paper grocery bag with doubled paper shoulder strap stapled on, worn backwards. See "On a Camping Trip" Hiking Pack project.)

Carrier takes the letters to the post office.

Other possible players:
cashier who sells stamps
sorter who sorts letters

Variation:
Add service station and garage for mail truck repair and fill-up; larger vehicle or wagon for cross-country delivery of boxes or bundles of mail; a scale, for weighing packages at post office; even a scanner (a cardboard box to pass the mail through) if mail safety has been a concern to your children's families.

Postal Sorting

Have families save old envelopes.

Color dot the envelopes with three to five different colors.

Mix the letters in a paper grocery bag.

Let either a small group or an individual child sort letters into boxes or bins with corresponding colored dots.

Remix to repeat for the next child or group.

Variation:

Add ink pad and stamp.

Each time a child sorts the letters, he may stamp the back of the letter, before placing it in the box.

Mail

Let your group's interests and contacts dictate where you send a letter or package. Examples:

Send a letter to a child who has moved away.

Write Mr. Rogers.

Write a thank you letter to the city parks and recreation department for the new swings in your park.

Letters can be flat 8 1/2″ × 11″, or they can be written on:

a long roll of adding tape

a folded piece of butcher paper

individual strips of paper, packed in a box

pieces of cardboard or construction paper, any size and shape

Make writing/letters/mailing fun!

Follow up: If possible, take children with you to the mailbox, or better yet, to the post office to mail the letter themselves.

Skippety on Letters to Freddy

I mailed a letter
to Freddy on Tuesday.
The next Tuesday
I got a letter back.
I'd asked if Freddy
would like to come visit.
His letter said
that he would.

So I mailed a letter
to Freddy on Wednesday.
The next Wednesday
I got a letter back.
I'd asked if he'd bring
his jump rope and marbles.
His letter said
that he would.

I mailed a letter
to Freddy on Thursday.
The next Thursday
I got a letter back.
I'd asked if Freddy
would like to go swimming.
His letter said
that he would.

I mailed a letter
to Freddy on Friday.
The next Friday
I got a letter back.
I'd asked if Freddy
would like to have pizza.
His letter said
that he would.

continued

Skippety on Letters to Freddy
(continued)

I mailed a letter
to Freddy on Saturday.
The next Saturday
I got a letter back.
I'd asked if he wanted
to play with my puppy.
His letter said
that he would.

I wrote a letter to Freddy
on Sunday,
and I mailed it on Monday.
Here's what I asked:
"FREDDY! WHEN ARE YOU COMING?"

Project

Make a Stamp

Bring in a variety of canceled stamps for the children to look through. Show them how some stamps are pictures of actual people or places, while other stamps are artists' drawings.

 Cut small squares or rectangles with pinking shears. Let children color their own stamps with fine-point markers or pens. Use them for gluing on pretend mail.

Let children who are interested in the above process draw in a three-inch square on typing paper, in black ink. Cut out with pinking shears. Reduce their drawing at a copy machine, and then copy a few of the small images into a row. This gives one more visual insight into how stamps are made. If you have a machine at school, let the children help you reduce and copy the drawing.

Real Estate Salesperson

Preparing Houses for Sale

Water table, set up with sand and:

a row of small cardboard boxes for houses

small "For Sale" signs

sections of straws for pipes

poster paint

small cars

small digging machinery

twigs, paper flowers, paper bushes

small squares of paper for roofing

Salesperson and property manager decide which houses need fixing before they can be sold:

landscaping

painting

roofing

new plumbing placed under foundation

Either the "salespeople" or "home repair crew" carry out the work.

Skippety on Houses

Which house would you buy?
Red, blue, or green?
You like the brown house?
The prettiest you've seen?

I like that bright house,
old, sturdy, strong.
I'd live in that light house
all my life long.

Imaginative Play

Selling Houses

phone
marker pens
newspaper ads
old copy of house listings book
real estate sales forms
briefcase (cereal box with handle)
phone book
calculator
laptop computer (cardboard box)

"For Sale" signs
Children may enjoy putting a "For Sale" sign up on your school or center, and play act the process of showing and selling it. They can also create a pretend town, in which houses come up for sale.

Neighborhood Mural

butcher paper mural
various sizes of construction paper
yellow paint in shallow trays
blocks, for block printing
collected materials for painting with (twigs, sprigs, popsicle sticks, etc.)
charcoal, green, and gray paint, in cups

Children glue up houses out of selected construction paper.
The windows can be added, using block prints. (Dipping the blocks in yellow paint and printing onto the house.)
Roofs may be painted on with collected materials.

Variation: Add rows of flowers and trees, printed on with any washable object.

Buying and Selling

Designate a certain area as the Neighborhood.
Each child pretends to be a House, and takes a place somewhere in the Neighborhood.
One child is chosen as the Buyer. The Buyer goes up to a House of his choosing. The buyer says "Is this house for sale?"
If the House answers "No," the Buyer goes to another House and repeats the question. (All Houses must be asked, before Buyer can return to a House. A House may only say "No" once to each Buyer.)
If the House answers "Yes," all the other Houses start chanting:
"Five hundred dollars and two cents
and three cents
and four cents
and five cents. Sold!"
While they're chanting, the Houses all over the room stay in their places, but they jump and wave and try to make the House that is For Sale laugh. If the House that is For Sale laughs, then the "deal falls through." The Buyer trades places with a different House and the House that was For Sale becomes part of the Neighborhood again.
If the House doesn't laugh before the Neighborhood Houses say "Sold!" that person gets to become the Buyer. Repeat.

Weaver Finch on Houses

Come gather round and I'll tell you a story.

Once there was a woman and a man who lived in a medium-size town. Their names were Harriet and Henry Holmes. The Holmeses loved houses. They also loved people. That's why they were so good at their work, selling houses.

Whenever a new family came to town looking for a house to buy, people would send them to the Holmeses. Harriet and Henry would have the family over for dinner. During dinner, the Holmeses asked the newcomers all kinds of questions. "Do you like trees and birds? Do you like to see out your windows, or do you like to be nestled in behind some bushes? Do you need a garage? A basketball hoop? An eating nook?" The Holmeses asked all these questions, and more.

The next day the Holmeses would take the new family to see just two or three houses that were for sale. Each of the houses had almost everything the family wanted. The Holmeses were great at matching houses to people.

The Holmeses sold the Farmers a big country house where they could grow corn and raise pigs in the garden shed. The Holmeses sold the Littles a teeny house by the town pond. Lily Little loved listening to the frogs.

What kind of house would they pick for the Woodmans? _____

What about the Belles? _____

What about the Carpenters? _____

What other kinds of houses do you think the Holmeses had listed for sale? _____

Who do you think they matched to each of those houses? _____

People loved buying houses from the Holmeses.

Finch, three, two, one. This story is done.

Scuba Diver

Weaver Finch on Scuba Diving Buddies

Come gather round and I'll tell you a story.

There once was a girl and a boy who loved to scuba dive.
They always dove together because when swimming, buddies are best.
But before they dove they had to get ready.
They put on their wet suits.
They put on their wet suits and their weight belts.
They put on their wet suits, their weight belts, and their diver's watches.
They put on their wet suits, their weight belts, their diver's watches, and finally their masks, fins, and snorkels.
The boy and the girl were ready.
They walked backwards down to the shore, and kept on walking backwards until they were up to their waists in the water.
Then, under the water they dove. Of course they swam together, because when swimming, buddies are best.
And oh what wonders they saw!
Can you guess what the boy and the girl saw underwater? _____ (Example: fish of specific colors and shapes, coral, oysters, eels, kelp, octopus, sea anemones, starfish)

Finch, three, two, one. This story is done.

Active Song

Oystering

(See the Appendix for the song sheet.)

	(Hold hands in a circle.)
Oystering, oystering,	(Rise on tiptoes while bringing hands up towards center of circle; still holding, let hands fall to sides.)
We will go an oystering.	(Repeat above motions, and let go this time when hands fall to sides.)
Dive down into the	(Hold own hands above head with thumbs linked;
cool green sea	dive to a squat.)
And pull up an oyster for you and me.	(Pull a pretend oyster; stand and hold in hand towards center of circle.)

Repeat.

Experiment

Scuba Diving Pairs

Set up water table with clear cool water.

If you have plastic scuba divers, great! If you don't, use two rectangular plastic blocks and call them the scuba divers.

With a wooden spoon, a water bottle with sprayer, and a wire gravy plunger, let two children at a time make currents to move the divers around.

Add smaller floating items, for fish. Add a plastic boat, or a styrofoam tray, for a diving platform.

Snack

Ocean Bowls

In individual bowls, scoop blueberry yogurt for the ocean.
Put in fish crackers and alfalfa sprouts as vegetation.

Used Car
Salesperson

Used Car Lot

small cars
car lot (a piece of cardboard sets it off from rest of the table)
triangle paper flags (strung on yarn, suspended between straws stuck upright in chunks of styrofoam)
Tinker Toys or other building set for making sales building
thimbles or little cups of water for car washing
teeny sponges
play money
cash register

Spare Tire Cookies

Prepare sugar cookie dough (substituting honey for half the amount of sugar, if desired).

Add food coloring (drops of red, blue, and green make light gray).

Roll and cut with doughnut cutters.

Bake as per recipe. Be sure *an adult* puts the cookie sheets in and out of the oven. Cool.

Skippety on Selling Cars

Come buy a car
on Used Car Mile.
Come buy a car
that's just your style.

Do you want the red one?
Or maybe the blue?
We've got just the
right car for you.

Take a test drive
in a car today.
Then come back tomorrow
Ready to pay.

Game

Used Cars

Partition off a car lot. Place a "stop sign" about 15 feet away from the edge of the lot.

One-half of the children are parked cars in the lot.

The others line up as customers.

To begin with, the teacher might want to be the Owner. As the children learn the game, a child can be chosen as Car Lot Owner.

The first customer comes to the Owner, saying "I'd like to test drive a _____(color)_____(make). (e.g., a blue Subaru)

The Owner gets one of the parked car children who's wearing something of that color.

The child who is the car positions herself in the wheelbarrow pose, with hands on ground. The customer takes up her feet.

They "drive" to the stop sign. (Younger children can stand, with the car in front, the customer putting hands on waist of the car. They walk together with the customer steering.)

Used Cars
(continued)

If they make it to the stop sign without falling, the customer pays the owner with pretend money, and the car and customer sit together in a line behind the stop sign.

If the car breaks down, the two trade places, and try again to make it to the stop sign. If they can't, they return to the customer line and lot. (The next time out, the children can use the modified version above, to be sure to make it to the stop sign.)

Repeat until all children have had a turn.

Weaver Finch on Buying Cars

Come gather round and I'll tell you a story.

Once, a long time ago, I decided I needed a new car. The one I had kept breaking down. So I drove with my children into the city. We looked at a Chevrolet. We looked inside and looked under the hood. Then the salesperson started up the car. I said I'd like to drive the Chevrolet. We all got in, and we drove around, and when we got back to the lot, I said, "I don't know. . . ."

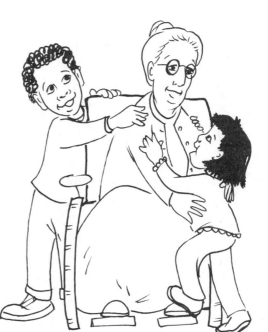

Just then we saw a friend of ours. _____ (a child in your group) said "Have you looked at a _____ (make of car)?" So we looked at a _____. We looked inside and looked under the hood. Then the salesperson started up the car. I said I'd like to drive the _____. We all got in, and we drove around, and when we got back to the lot, I said, "I don't know. . . ."

(Repeat, giving each child a turn. Some groups will know enough car makes for each to choose a new kind of car; other groups may need to reuse some names. The children will soon be reciting each step with you.)

Finch, three, two, one. This story is done.

Weather Forecaster

Rainbow

a grab bag
cards, each with a picture of one type of weather:
(For family literacy, you'll also want to write the names below the pictures.)

sunshine	clouds	wind
rain	thunder	lightning

On the back of the sunshine and rain cards are two halves of a rainbow. Side by side, they make a whole.

Show each of the cards to the children. Have them identify the weather pictures. Show sun and rain together. Show how these make a rainbow.

Put the cards in the grab bag. Shake them up.

Have everyone stand in a circle.

Take the bag around the outside of the circle. Have two children, standing adjacent, each draw out a card. They face the center of the circle and act out the weather. The children in the rest of the circle call out the names of the cards being acted out. But, if sun and rain are acted out, the children call out "Rainbow!"

Rainbow
(continued)

When there's a rainbow, the two children who drew sun and rain hold up their hands in an arch, and, starting from their left, the circle of children winds under the rainbow and back to their places in the circle.

The game resumes with the grab bag being shaken again and taken around the outside of the circle to the next two children.

Mapping the Weather

Hang a U.S. map on your lowest bulletin board, or mount it on cardboard within reach of the children.

Have a number of small cards with weather symbols in a container below the map. (Examples: rain, sunshine, snow, wind, clouds, thunder and lightning, hail)

Let the children and their families report on changes in the weather all over the country, by pinning up symbols of weather conditions that affect their family. For example, "My sister goes to school in Boston. She said it's snowing."

Clouds

light blue construction paper
gray, pink, yellow, and black paints
cotton balls and glue
You might first want to observe the sky with the children on several different weather days.

Then let children experiment with these materials to create how they want to depict the sky. They may want to make more than one picture, since their pictures will change quickly, as they add color and texture.

Hang these on the ceiling, in clumps of fair, fine, and foul weather.

Weather Watch

Go outdoors with the children to find a suitable weather station. If possible, it should be out of the reach of passing animals.

Wind Meter

Materials:

a 1-inch-wide ribbon, about a foot long (plastic, if you have it, but cloth will do)

a long dowel

a couple of tacks

Push the dowel into the ground. Fold the ribbon back about an inch at one end. Tack that end of the ribbon to the top of the dowel.

Label the four directions at ground level. An easy way to label the directions: cut a slit to the center of a recycled For Sale sign. At the center, cut out a circle the size of the dowel. Slip the For Sale sign, upside down, around the dowel. Write the directions on the blank side of the sign. Of course, you may also label on blocks of wood or any way that works for you and your weather spot. If you're in an arid climate, you might write in chalk on the playground.

When "reading" the wind, remember that the wind is identified by the direction from which it comes. If the ribbon is blowing out to the south, you would pronounce it a north wind.

Thermometer

Mount an outdoor thermometer at a level where the children can at least see the reading go up and down. Place it by something you can write on. Mark areas that you would consider COLD, WARM, and HOT alongside the thermometer, relevant to your area and season of the year. Children shouldn't be expected to read the exact degrees, but they can note the temperature in general terms.

Scientific observation at the preschool age must be fun, using skills they're able to master. With these three simple words, and gradations of color from white, to pink, to red, all children can "read" the temperature.

Weather Watch
(continued)

Rain Gauge

Tape a plastic or wooden stick inside a plastic container to measure precipitation. Decide for your children how you want to "read" the gauge. You may need to adapt your measure to clearly written lines for 1-, 2-, 3-inches apart, but with no marks in between. Children can "read" the precipitation as almost up to the 1, only halfway to the 1, hardly any, etc. For older children you could add 1/4, 1/2, 3/4, etc. designations in between the inch marks that would give more precise measurements but would be easier to read than an actual ruler.

Weaver Finch on Weather

Come gather round and I'll tell you a story.

Once on my fifth birthday I woke up to a dancingly sunshiny day. I put on my shorts and a T-shirt and skittered downstairs to breakfast. Mother always made blueberry muffins on birthday mornings. Oh were they good!

After breakfast I went out to play. But very soon the wind came up. It blew my hair right into my mouth. It blew my new puppy off the ground. It blew and blew and blew! So I went back inside to put on _____.

(The story continues, letting the children help decide what Weaver Finch wore with each change in the weather. After every change, send her back outside, only to have her play interrupted again with rain, thunder, hail, snow, or sunshine. The children will help you have her changes include putting on or taking off clothes.)

The weather kept changing the whole day long. After dinner Mother brought out my birthday cake. I was so tired from changing clothes all day long, that I fell asleep SPLAT! right in my cake.

Finch, three, two, one. This story is done.

Web Page Designer

Imaginative Play

Internet Design Business

Create an adjoining "room" to the home corner. The mom or the dad can pretend to go to work in the home office.

Add:

either a real computer, desk, and chair or a pretend computer made out of a box, with a small box keyboard

pictures on the wall of happy clients (drawn by the children)

a conference table (for visiting clients)

pencils and a pad of paper

a nerf basketball hoop and ball (for breaks)

a teapot and pretend cups

You might also have a baby and baby bed in the office. Often parents who work out of the home do so while taking care of an infant.

Web Design

For use with technologically precocious preschoolers or school-age children in your care. Talk about what service the Web Page Designer provides. A Web Page Designer helps a person, organization, or company by putting particular pictures and words that describe them, in layers of "pages" on the computer screen.

Go online, if possible, to look at Mr. Rogers' Web site, for instance (http://pbskids.org/rogers/), so children can see the work and choices a web designer is involved with. Look at the difference between Mr. Rogers' Web site and any other Web site of your children's interest, for instance, the Oregon Zoo in Portland, Oregon (www.oregonzoo.org).

Creating Web Pages

This activity can allow children who are well-versed in computers at home to explore Web site development, even if you don't have a computer and design program available. If you do, all the better!

Get a lid, such as that on office supply boxes.

Have the children identify a group to put "on the web." Your school or child care facility would be fun, for example, if you're not already located online.

Begin with a cover page. Let the children cut and paste pictures, words, and other images onto an 11×17-inch sheet of paper.

Next have them make a list of what will go onto the Web site.

the activities
the children
the adults
the location
the various rooms

You see how easy it is to show children what goes on a Web site. And the order that images are revealed is entirely up to the decisions the designer makes with the client.

Let groups of children work on each of the pages.

Put the pages in the box in the same order as the children have decided to list them.

Attach a cord and a computer mouse facsimile to the box lid. Make a paper arrow to represent the cursor.

continued

Creating Web Pages
(continued)

Quickly sketch a home page that shows an image for each page they've made. Show the children that when they click on one image on the home page (using the paper arrow), the computer sorts through the pages to locate the information on the selected page. Demonstrate, by bringing the selected page to the top. Repeat, showing all their pages.

If you have a computer available, invite a Web site designer in to show the children, very simplistically, what he does in his job.

Winger on Web Design

(Pick and choose which, if any, of Winger's thoughts you want to share with your group. You may offer this info in tiny bites, as interest arises. Of course, if you're honoring a parent whose business takes place on the Internet, discussion/demystification may well be in order.)

I'll tell you what I think about computers and the Internet. I think it's pretty strange. Do you know even when my brother was a little guy, we didn't have anything like the computers we have today. Back then, one computer would fill a whole room. Now computers can fit in your hand. When Weaver Finch was growing up, computers hadn't even been thought up yet.

When Weaver Finch was growing up, people wrote on paper, with a pencil or pen. Families were lucky to have typewriters to make their writing neat. Not very many people owned typewriters. My aunt was a writer before computers were around. You should've seen the wastebasket by her desk. It was always overflowing with crumpled papers because if she made a mistake, or if she wanted to change even one sentence, she had to start all over. It took my aunt hours . . . well, days and weeks and months actually, to type up the pages for a book.

Winger on Web Design
(continued)

So it was really something when computers started being used. At first, people were thrilled that they could do simple writing in much less time. If they messed up, an easy cut and paste on the computer screen would take care of the problem. Businesses used computers too to keep track of all the money they earned and the money they owed other people. Stores starting using computers to keep track of the things they had for sale. Doesn't it amaze you that just a few years ago, no one had even heard of a computer, and now they're everywhere?

If Weaver Finch finds the computer hard to get used to, imagine what she thinks about the Internet. Now the Internet's a whole new thing, but it isn't a thing actually, not that we can touch. Stores use computers to be sure they have enough things to sell, and now they can sell on the Internet, too. But it's so strange. There isn't actually a store on the Internet, not a building kind of store. An Internet store is just a list of things, or pictures of things, that you press or highlight on the computer screen. The things are all kept in a warehouse. The only time you actually see the things for sale on the Internet, is when the delivery person pulls up to your door.

The Internet made new places for people to work. The web designers make up the pictures and words that show on the computer screens to tell about the stores. Oh, web designers work on Web sites that tell about more than stores. They can tell about parks, and cities, and people, and music, and animals. There's stuff on the Internet about everything! So the web designers work on making the pages on the Internet look really good so people enjoy coming to that Web site. (Only the pages aren't the kind we can touch or turn either. They're just pictures on the computer, pictures inside pictures.) The Web site's a place, but it's only on the computer screen. Isn't that amazing when you think about it!

Window Washer

Washing Windows

On a warm day, let the children set up a washing business.

It's doubtful that you have a window on your building that children can safely wash. *Do not set children up with squeegees that can be knocked through a window.* How about the passenger windows on an older car? Or adapt the activity to a house washing, rather than window washing business. Even a pretend house will do. This is imaginative play.

buckets
sponge
squeegee
play checks
receipt pad and pen
trikes and wagons for hauling equipment
dry cloths, for afterwards

See Clearly

If you happen to have a set of plastic mirrors as part of your self-esteem work, let children use some of the same equipment indoors for washing plastic mirrors. Before they wash the mirrors, let them rub their hands with hand lotion. (Be sure you have a hypoallergenic brand if any of your children have sensitive skin. Either skip this activity or have a substitute for a child who has skin allergies.) The children can make fingerprints on the mirrors. Then their "business" can get the mirrors clean again.

More Washing

Gather all the rubber balls you can find. Using a big tub, let the children wash the balls.

From a child's viewpoint, washing is fun. What else can be washed? Indoor table and chair set? Outdoor lawn furniture? A fence? (as long as there aren't sharp pieces or wood splinters)

Washing

The windows are dirty.	*(Shake your head.)*
What can be seen?	*(Look wide-eyed, straight ahead.)*
Squirt on the water.	*(Pretend squirt with a spray bottle.)*
Round wipe them clean.	*(Pretend wipe in a circular motion, as if on a window.)*
The windows look better.	*(Nod head.)*
Now don't you feel good?	*(Hands on hips.)*
We washed the windows.	*(Pretend wipe, in a circular motion, with both hands.)*
I knew that we could.	*(Pat your back.)*

Use this rhyme only if it makes sense with what they have actually accomplished. If it wasn't safe to allow them to wash windows, you might want to skip the action rhyme.

Weaver Finch on Window Washing

Come gather round and I'll tell you a story.

Now there was, in and out of time, a mother with seven bright children. They were called _____ (name seven children in your group), _____, _____, _____, _____, _____, and _____.

The mother washed windows for her living. She drove a nine-passenger van with racks on top for her ladders and squeegees. Mom worked all day by herself. But she scheduled the tallest buildings for the last job of each day. She'd pick up the oldest children at school, and they'd go with her to hold the long ladder so she could climb up safely. When they got home after that last job, the children washed the sponges and wrung them to dry. Mom took a few minutes of quiet time in her garden while the children tidied up. Dinners and evenings they spent all together.

Grandpa Friday took care of the little ones during the day. He let them help him make big burbling stews. And they made homemade bread to go with the greens from Mom's garden.

The children, _____, _____, _____, _____, _____, _____, and _____, were proud of their mother's business. Mom was proud of her children. And she was sure glad to have Grandpa Friday's help. Of course, Grandpa Friday loved being part of all the goings-on in their big family.

Finch, three, two, one. This story is done.

Section

Changes

Changes are stressful, no matter whether a change for the better or the worse. Unexpected changes jolt even more. Children are said to be adaptable, flexible, and able to handle change. They bound back . . . in the long run. But in the short run, teachers are apt to be questioning, "What is going on in the child's life to cause her to act this way?"

Some children move relatively smoothly through the unexpected. Others are shaken; they fit and sputter in much the same way as they do before coming down with a fever. And their distress spatters about them, affecting everyone they come in contact with.

Yet change is inevitable. The activities in this section will help you to tune in to children through the planned changes. And when something unexpected arises, you'll have activities to choose from or modify, to immediately validate that child's feelings and to help him cope.

Also keep in mind, it is not our place as teachers and caregivers to have a stake in the changes that occur in families' lives. The activities here provide validation for changes that do impact children's lives, not approval *or* disapproval for such changes. The point is to allow recognition for "what is up" for children, and to do so for all children, regardless of their experience.

A number of the topics listed here indicate a possibly dysfunctional family life. It's important to remember not to take on the role of family therapist. Projects about other changes such as divorce, death, and remarriage all will bring up feelings in the child. They may also bring up feelings within you if you have experienced these changes yourself. The point of the activities is to acknowledge the child, allow the child to feel heard, and enable the child to move through feelings in acceptable, nondestructive activities. Being heard alone can dissipate negative feelings, even if nothing can be done to alter the change in the child's life. Remember, if you are using Winger as a puppet to help children express their concerns or fears, do allow *the child* to speak, so Winger can reflect back the feelings. Don't use Winger to tell the child *what* to feel.

Experts in child therapy tell us though, to be sure we don't expect preschoolers to be able to verbalize their feelings very well. Most are just not able to say what they feel. Our "hearing" ought also take the form of being patiently present when they bounce and bounce on a mattress or throw a doll against the wall or pound a pillow relentlessly. We can't expect children who have undergone trauma to be able to clean up their feelings. We can create situations where they will move feelings through their bodies in safe and tolerable ways.

One particularly easy and extremely successful arena for children to process change can be found in the ordinary "home corner." Imaginative play, whether it be in the midst of your child-size kitchen, or table-size play with people and objects in miniature, allows children to work through their feelings. You can add props, such as I did when our family was in an accident involving a deer. Letting the children in my home care replay the deer leaping in front of the car, helped my own daughter and others to process the scary feelings associated with such accidents. Add hats, coats, or other *safe* objects associated with the child's experience to the traditional home corner. If the experience happened outside the home, you might replace the home corner with another setting for a time, until the children are "finished" with their feelings. A firehouse might be useful after a fire, or a school building, if your children are affected, as were some in our area recently, by an unidentified rash. Add a doctor's kit and a health department investigator's props to the "school." The more the children can play about their real life experiences, the more they will move through their worries and fears.

Protective intervention at home may be indicated at times, due to dysfunctional family dynamics. If you are aware that disagreements in a child's home escalate into physical abuse, you have a clear mandate to report information to Child Protective Services. Use common sense, the guidelines of your school or child care center, and local and state laws when applicable to direct your responses.

No matter whether the situation requires outside assistance or is simply a situation for the family to get through, we can use these activities to help the child deal with the churnings within. Sometimes we'll want to be there with soothing, affirming projects. Other times it'll be more important to encourage a child to release angers and frustrations by hitting an object in a quickly devised game, before the child hits a child. The more in tune we are with our children's lives outside the classroom, the more able we will be to intuitively pick the right activity.

With all activities, we try to set boundaries ahead of time, so the children know the acceptable parameters of their play. When responding to emotionally charged changes in a child's life, we need to be even more careful to be clear beforehand. Feelings are bound to come up as a child moves through the activity. It's important for a child to know at what point she will need to pull in the controls. If we've set limits beforehand, then our monitoring need only be gentle reminders instead of a series of after-the-fact instructions, halting and correcting the child's behavior.

We walk a fine line here, because we also want the activity to be the child's. Protect the child and others first. Then focus simply on setting out materials or setting the stage, without dictating how the child will make use of them, *except in regards to safety.* Always remember, with projects the experience matters more than a product. We can hope and expect that the children will transform our ideas into activities uniquely meaningful to each of them.

Car Accident

Note:
The following activities would suit a child who was in an accident that did not involve a death. Turn to "Death of a Family Member," or "Tumultuous Times," then adapt activities to deal with such trauma.

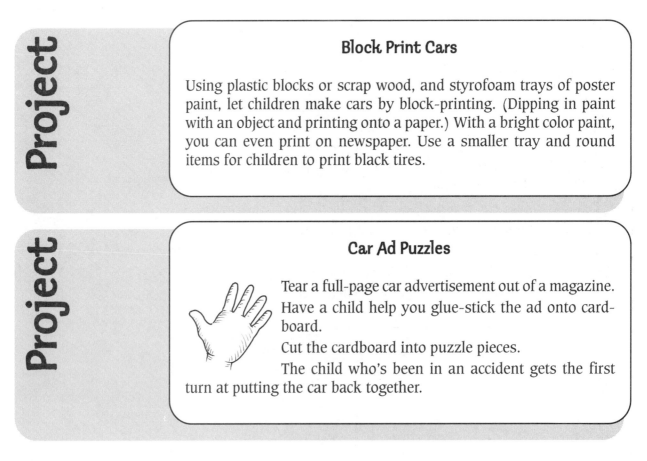

Project

Block Print Cars

Using plastic blocks or scrap wood, and styrofoam trays of poster paint, let children make cars by block-printing. (Dipping in paint with an object and printing onto a paper.) With a bright color paint, you can even print on newspaper. Use a smaller tray and round items for children to print black tires.

Project

Car Ad Puzzles

Tear a full-page car advertisement out of a magazine. Have a child help you glue-stick the ad onto cardboard.

Cut the cardboard into puzzle pieces.

The child who's been in an accident gets the first turn at putting the car back together.

Revisiting Accident, Table Size

Use whatever toys you have available for reenacting the accident.
cars
trucks
toy deer
trees
houses
road made of blocks or paper
small stop signs
ice

 Add fire truck, ambulance, aide car if you have them, or put paper Red Cross or other symbol on a vehicle you do have.

Cars on the Road

Hang a length of paper on a wall, at child's height. Draw a road on the paper.

 Copy 4-inch outlines of a car (either drawn freehand or traced from an advertisement) onto a piece of recycled file folder, or something of that weight.

Let children cut out the cars. Color if they wish.

Put tape rolls on the backs of the cars.

Blindfold one child at a time, beginning with the child in the accident. Turn child around slowly.

Child holds up car cut-out, with the tape rolls facing away from her.

Child moves forward, trying to place the car on the road.

Take turns, each child with his own car.

The child who has been in the accident may rearrange the cars on the road when you're finished with the game.

Activity

Spotting Safe Drivers

Decide if this activity matches the circumstances. Often children are involved in accidents due to careless driving. If you know that the driver at fault was the child's parent, you will not want to do this activity; it won't help the child to be accusing the parent or adding to the parent's guilt. If, however, you know that another car's driver did not adhere to safe driving rules, this activity could be very reassuring.

Be sure not to lecture on safe driving though. You don't even need to comment about how many safe drivers there are on the roads. Children internalize through observations such as this. If you do comment, be sure your underlying message validates the child's experience *that not all drivers are safe.* This exercise isn't meant to talk the child out of his feelings, but to offer an alternative to staying scared.

Let the children help you make cut-outs of different colored cars, two times the number of children. Put all of these in a basket.

Take a walk with the group with you carrying the basket filled with cars. Be on the lookout for safe drivers. Whenever a child spots a safe driver, the child gets to take a car of the same color out of the basket.

On the walk back, let the child who was in the accident hold the basket. Let the children look for safe drivers again, and when a safe driver's car is a color match to one of their cars, they put it back in the basket. Some groups can care for each other to this degree. If you don't think your children can relinquish their cars for the purpose of the activity, skip this step.

Winger on Accidents

One morning we were on our way to my caregiver, and there was ice on the road. Poppa put on the brakes, but we didn't stop. It was kind of like we were in slow motion, going sideways. We slid right into a ditch. The car tipped. It felt like it might turn over. My heart was racing. It was hard to un-buckle my seat belt, because I was all shaky. There weren't any other cars on the road, so we had to walk in the freezing rain to call a tow truck to pull us out.

I don't like accidents. Course I don't think anybody does.

Another time I was going to the ocean with my grandpa and grandma. A deer jumped out in front of us. Grandpa couldn't help it; he hit the deer. Grandma kept hugging me and hugging me. We had our seat belts on, so nobody got hurt. (The deer did though; that was sad.) That accident was scariest because it happened so fast.

Weaver Finch on Accidents

Come gather round and I'll tell you a story.

(Throwing up your hands.) So what's a mother to do if the kids are screaming, the horns are honking, and a wad of paper sails by her head? She might get in an accident.

(Throwing up your hands.) So what's a daddy to do if the baby's crying, the rain is roaring, and the dog is climbing on the steering wheel? He might get in an accident.

So what's a nana to do if the kids are punching each other and a big wind is blowing paper off the street onto the windshield? She might get in an accident.

You know what? If you're in a car, and it's noisy like that . . . Stop! Tell your brother or sister or friend to STOP! Have everybody take three deep breaths . . . and let the driver drive.

Otherwise, you know what might happen? _____ You're right. An accident. The kind where people or animals get hurt.

You can help your family to *not* get in an accident . . . Let the driver drive.

Finch, three, two, one. This story is done, without any accidents!

New Baby

Note:

I am offering as many activities, thereby seemingly placing equal emphasis, on the birth of a child's pet as on the birth or adoption of a sibling. Consider that when a new sibling comes on the scene, the older child will be having to deal with the displacement of position in the family, the time and attention devoted to the newcomer, the cuteness factor, etc. While the birth of a sibling is a momentous occasion in a child and family's life, let's not aggravate the adjustment by adding too much attention.

You may have children in your care though, such as a seven-year-old who has really looked forward to having another child in the family, who would benefit from available activities. Grandparents, or other adults in the child's life, might appreciate the opportunity to help that child give voice and form to the excitement.

Refer to the following activities to allow the child to positively acknowledge the event. Use your own judgment whether the particular child will benefit or not from activity response. While there are plenty of ideas listed here, be especially sure not to overload a child regarding the new baby.

All activities around New Baby need to acknowledge that babies can be born or adopted ("born from the heart instead of the tummy" as Rosey and Barbara say). Please adapt these and Family Member's Birthday activities to suit the adoption of an older child.

Imaginative Play

New Babies

baby doll
doll crib
diapers
small rocking chair
baby blanket
baby clothes
baby bottle, doll-size and child-size

Children with baby siblings often revert to being the baby. You may have to resolve whether it's okay for a child to put the bottle in her mouth. Will the children take turns being baby? And do you have a way to wash/sterilize the bottle between "babies?" If not, eliminate a child-size baby bottle from the play.

Think ahead as you equip/set the stage for new baby play. Does the mother of a newborn in your care breast-feed her baby? If so, you will not want to encourage the child himself to be the baby. Rather, you can allow breast-feeding by having a receiving blanket to cover the baby doll when nursing. Don't be surprised if the older sibling who is a boy acts out the mother's role. The point of imaginative play is to let the child play out his feelings. If he is exploring the event from the mother's standpoint, all the better.

Activity

Visiting Nurse

Have a pediatric nurse visit your classroom, with a brief lesson on baby care. The self-esteem of the child with the new sibling will be bolstered, because he will be familiar with the topic. The instruction might also prevent an accident.

Baby Biscuits

Pat a biscuit out of prepared biscuit dough. Then roll extra dough into a little ball.

Place the "baby" in the center of the big brother or sister biscuit.

Each child can make his/her own, or the expecting child can prepare snacks for everyone.

Skippety on Babies

Loo li oh lay li oo.
We have a new baby.
How about you?

Loo li oh lay li ie.
I'll burp the baby
and sing "Lullaby."

Li li oh lay li. . .ack!
Baby spit up on me.
Quick! Take her [him] back!

Celebrating

Perhaps during the week of the baby's birth, or when indicated by the older sibling in your care, celebrate.

Pass out musical instruments.

Stand up, using musical instruments as you chant:

Let's celebrate the birthday of a baby.
Let's celebrate the birthday of a baby.
Let's celebrate the birthday of a baby.
And hop and jump and clap!   *(hop, jump, and clap)*

Repeat (using new motions at the end if you like, such as spin and spin around).

Nesting

In the spring, the anticipation of new life is recognized throughout the animal world. There's a conceptual stretch in this activity. Can you convey the similarity between birds laying eggs, then *waiting* until they hatch, and people having babies growing inside a woman's tummy, then *waiting* for the birth or adoption? This activity can be a fun one for children waiting for springtime siblings.

Cut a large box (washing machine size) down to 8-inches tall. Either gather dried grasses with the children, or bring in enough hay to cover the bottom of the box. Let the children make it into a nest. Either use the largest plastic egg you have, or approximate an egg shape with a plastic frosting container.

Let children take turns sitting on the egg to keep it warm. The expecting child can help decide what should be placed over the egg to keep it warm through the night. When you're ready for the egg to hatch, cut it open one morning before the children arrive, and place a chick inside. (If you don't have a toy chick, you can make a chick out of a yellow yarn pom pom, gluing on wings and eyes and a beak.) Then let all the children make their own chicks.

Note:
Hay fever in some children may require you to move this activity outdoors (if your weather allows). Devise an alternate treat for the child who can't nest.

Winger on New Baby

Here's what I remember about new babies: At first, all I heard when my baby sister arrived was "baby this" and "baby that" and "Isn't your baby cute?" And "Aren't you a proud little man to have such a cute little baby?"

Well, she's not *my* baby, and I was tired of that baby business. Sometimes I wanted my old family back! Sometimes I even cried pretend, "Whaaa, whaa!" just like a baby.

Weaver Finch on Winger's Feeling

I was an only child. I always wanted a little brother or sister. So I don't think I can really understand how angry Winger felt. Does anyone here know how Winger felt?

Weaver Finch on Babies

Come gather round and I'll tell you a story.

You know, a long time ago, before I got in this wheelchair, before my chin skin flapped, before I got white hair . . . a long, long time ago I had a baby. People said she was my spittin' image.

Now my baby was born in the spring. Daffodils were in bloom. And hyacinths. And lilacs. Flowers bloomed all around our house. I thought about how my baby would grow up and blossom just like a flower. So I called my baby Tulip.

Some people name their children after relatives. Some people give children their own names. Some people choose a name because they like the sound of it. If you decide to be a mother or father, what would you name your baby someday? _____ , _____, _____, etc.

Let's pretend all our babies lived together in a big flowered field. There was _____ (going around the group, let each child repeat the baby name they chose).

But the babies weren't happy. They needed brothers and sisters. Let's pretend they got brothers and sisters with names just like yours. So the babies had _____, _____, etc. for their brothers and sisters. All of the babies and the brothers and sisters rolled in the grass together, and giggled, of course. They ate a picnic campout, which was yummy, of course. And they slept together under the stars. And snored, of course.

Finch, three, two, one. This story is done.

Family Member's Birthday

Note:
Some families do not celebrate birthdays, and prefer their children not be present during celebrations at school. If you have families with such beliefs in your group, you will probably want to skip over this topic. The regular acknowledgement of the children's birthdays creates exclusion and logistic challenges enough.

Explain to helping parents and volunteers that I include family member's birthdays not with the expectation that you will honor all family members. These ideas simply give you more options in acknowledging families, in one way or another throughout the year.

"Look At Me" Book

Use a small premade book, one with only a few pages.

Ask children about the family member's favorite thing to do, favorite color, favorite food. Let the child draw and color or cut out pictures of these interests. Label each page as the child explains.

Tie a ribbon around the "present." Add a sticky note "Happy Birthday" with the child's signature or mark.

The idea's simple, takes only a few minutes, involves the child in literacy activity, and acknowledges family members.

Project

Skippety on Family Birthdays

Hippety bippety.
A birthday
at your house!
Hippety skip hooray!

Hippety bippety
a birthday
at your house.
What a bright, happy,
hip happy day!

For Birthdays

If fitting, print up this action rhyme for the child to share at home.
Practice with the child.

Happy, happy,	*(Squat down.)*
Birthday, birthday.	*(Stand up.)*
Happy	*(Squat down.)*
birthday	*(Stand up.)*
One, two, three.	*(Jump, jump, jump.)*

Repeat.

For a Birthday

Have the child cut out 1-inch circles in red, yellow, green, and blue paper, or have the child cut out four white circles and color.
Teach the game to the child:
You hold one of the circles in your hand, behind your back.

You say: "Guess which color
   is in my hand.
   Guess which color
   in all the land.
   Is it red, green,
   yellow, or blue?
   Guess which color
   I have for you.

The child guesses which color. Repeat until the color in your hand is guessed. Give the child that circle.
Repeat for all the circles.
The child can then take the game home, to be played with the birthday person. The child would recite your part and the birthday person would do the guessing. The child may not be able to remember the rhyme, so you can send home a copy and a message to have an older family member help review the rhyme before playing.

Party Favors

Cut thin strips of paper, in an assortment of colors.
Let the child roll these around a pencil.
The child can tape several curls to the top of a straw.
Let the child make and take home as many as are in his family, for colorful wands to shake at their party.
Package them in an envelope that you label "Party Shakers," and "Happy Birthday," with the birthday person's name.

Caring for an Aging Adult

Flowers for a Friend

When winter snows and cold temperatures make for dreary days, let children put together a flower pot for an older friend of their family:

construction paper, cut in thin strips

The children roll the strips tightly around a pencil, one at a time. The strips will curl.

The children glue the curls on the top of a straw or a thin piece of dowel.

Let the children make one or several.

Stick in small pot of dirt or in a bottle for a vase.

The children can take the gift to an older friend or relative they care for.

Alternate Bouquet

Let children wrap thick rug yarn around a large spool of thread and glue in place.

Have squares of tissue cut, in several colors.

Children gather sheets of tissue from the center, twisting a pipe cleaner to hold the core of each blossom together.

Place "flowers" in the spool vase.

Skippety on Caring

Look at the poems I found in a box of my grandmother's things:

Swing, Ring

Swing, ring, the wind chimes jingle.
What'll we plant now?
The weather's getting warmer.
Swing, ring, the wind chimes jingle.
You bring the trowels.
I've got the sack 'o peas.

Working on Wood

Light from the wrinkled garage
shines on the berry vines.
Inside,
the old man and his granddaughter
work together
in wood.

Woman in her Seventies

Woman in her seventies,
folded in the clover,
sharing her memories
with the barefoot boys.

Older/Younger Book

Using one of your premade small books, fill out several pages with the child.

Examples for what to put on the pages:

When my _____ (grandma, uncle . . .) was younger, she lived _____ (on a farm, in the city . . .).

When my _____ (older friend or relative) was younger, he played _____ (mumbledy-peg, horse shoes, stick ball . . .).

Then:

When I get older,

I'll _____ (learn to play cards) like _____.

When I get older, I'll _____ (learn to paint like my) _____ (relative or friend).

The child takes the book home to the older relative. Together they fill any of the sentences the child has left blank. They may need to get the help of another person in the household to write in their answers. The child adds illustrations wherever desired.

If possible, invite the child to bring the book back to school to read before he leaves it with his older adult friend or relative.

Remember When

Help the child draw a game route on a piece of cardboard. Make sure the spaces are large enough to easily accommodate two markers. Ask the child to name a special place that she has been with her older friend or relative. Let the child draw that special spot, or in some way identify the spot, as the end of the game.

Help the child make a spinner, using a smaller piece of cardboard and a brad.

Collect markers such as shells or rocks.

Play the game several times with the child.

Let the child take the game to teach to the older friend or relative.

Hospital Gift

Let the child make a pet to take to the relative or friend in the hospital.

small paper plate for head
snips of yarn for fur
magic marker or crayon for drawing on a face
paper tail and ears

(Even the process of making this "pet" may bring up talk of illness, death, and dying. Encourage the child to talk about his feelings as best he can. This giving provides a means of dealing with the illness and the possibility of death.)

Winger on Caring

Lots of times we go to see my Great Aunt Ruby. She can't remember things very well, so I tell her who I am. We take her cookies and pictures I've drawn for her. I don't mind visiting Aunt Ruby, but I don't like her turning me around and around to see how I've grown, 'specially when she can't remember me! I know that's not Aunt Ruby's fault though. She's just having trouble with her memory.

Is there anything you really don't like about being with an older friend or relative? _____

You know what I really think about caring though? Caring does make me feel good.

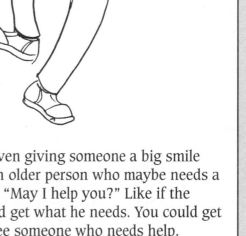

There are two ways that I like to care for older people. One is by just being kind in the world. Even giving someone a big smile can be a way of caring. Then sometimes I might see an older person who maybe needs a little help, like in a grocery store. So I ask that person, "May I help you?" Like if the older person can't reach to a high-up shelf, I fly up and get what he needs. You could get the adult you're with to reach the high things if you see someone who needs help.

continued

Winger on Caring
(continued)

The other way I like to care for older people is pretty easy. Every so often I make a list of all the older people I care about. That helps me remember to show them I care. I might draw my grandpa a picture or make Aunt Ruby a collage. Sometimes I go to their houses and pick up the fallen apples, or dust all the rungs on the chairs (those are hard to get to when you're older), or just play a game with them. You know, my heart always feels big inside, kind of like it's swollen up real warm, after I spend time with my older friends.

What do you do to show older people you care? _____
How do you feel afterwards? _____ (Questions like these focus on identifying feelings that aren't charged with great emotion. Ultimately this practice may help children move towards verbalizing their feelings in tougher situations.)

Weaver Finch on Caring for an Aging Friend or Relative

Come gather round and I'll tell you a story.

When I was younger, my Great Aunt Marna lived in a nursing home. Nowadays these helping places are called assisted living or care facilities. Aunt Marna never claimed to feel any better than "fair to middlin'." The caregivers were very kind though, even when Aunt Marna complained.

My great aunt always said what was on her mind. So when people talked to her loudly as if she couldn't hear, she would holler back, "I may be old, but I can hear you just fine!" When the visitors would ask things about my aunt, talking as if she wasn't there, my aunt would speak right up, "If you want to know what's going on, why don't you ask me?" And when new nurses or visitors would talk to my aunt like she was a baby, sometimes Aunt Marna would put her thumb in her mouth and go "Goo, goo, goo," just for fun.

Weaver Finch on Caring for an Aging Friend or Relative
(continued)

One thing that was difficult about being with Aunt Marna, she could get kind of gruff. She'd scowl at me when I'd come by after school and ask me "Where have you been!" It wasn't a question at all. She thought I had taken too long, when I wasn't even late. Aunt Marna would get mixed up about time. But as soon as she'd get herself straightened out, we'd play a game of cards. She was very impressed when I would win. I liked visiting Aunt Marna.

Finch, three, two, one. This story is done.

First Cold Spell
of the Year

Ice

Collect enough icicles or chunks of ice to fill your water table two or three times. Keep the extra ice outdoors, and bring it in to replace each melted batch.

In groups, let the children touch and pile and chip the icicles and sheets of ice. Since you've probably collected your ice at random outdoors, you'll need to set limits ahead of time, that the ice can be touched with fingers, but not with tongues. Skip the ice activity if your children can't abide by this agreement.

Add ice cubes and see if the children notice anything different about the two types of ice.

Sponge Painting

Let children paint construction paper dark blue. Let it dry. (Or use colored construction paper if you'd rather not wait.)

Set out trays with white poster paint, and an assortment of sponges.

You might want to ask if the children can make a picture of the first snowfall. Be sure not to demonstrate as that will fill their mind's eye with *your image* of the first snowfall. The value is in their getting to recreate nature's flurries, expressed in their own unique ways.

Cocoa Dip

Let the children each cut their bread slice with a small, 1 to 1 1/2″ round cookie cutter or what-have-you.

For each two rounds of bread, they will put one raisin in between. The children then pinch the edges of their bread together, so the raisin is encased.

Serve mugs of warm cocoa. The children may dip the rounds of bread in their cocoa, nibbling until they find the raisin.

You want to be sure to let the children assemble these so they know to watch for the raisin.

Do not serve to little ones who would choke on the raisin.

Ice House

Let children make a miniature igloo on a tray outdoors.

They can pack snow into trapezoid-shaped containers (ice cube trays, or plastic food containers).

Show them how to alternate the wider and narrower ends as they bonk the blocks out of the trays and stack them in a circle, layer upon layer.

The igloo can be brought in to the water table for a short time, for playing with small toy people and dogs.

Variation on Igloo

Have the children fill ice cube trays with water. Let them help you set some of the trays outside. Leave them to freeze. Have the children put the rest of the trays in the freezing compartment of the fridge.

You don't need to point out how things freeze. Let the children make their own observations about ice being made outdoors and ice forming in the refrigerator. They will take note, naturally, of which are frozen first.

Using the ice cubes from both "freezers," allow the children to build/explore with ice in a water table.

Skippety on the Cold

Brr, brr, brr, brr.
I need some fur, fur,
like a big bear bear
when it's cold.

Shiver, shiver, shiver, shiver.
Wouldn't go in the river river,
like a silver salmon salmon
when it's cold.

Chatter, chatter, chatter, chatter,
Screeching, knocking, clatter, clatter.
Like a hungry gray jay
when it's cold.

Whee! Yiiii! Hoo-ray!
Look at all the snow today.
Let's go out and play play
in the cold!

Winger, When It's Cold

Here's what I think about this cold spell: I think about the animals when it's cold. It's good they have fur and feathers to keep them warm. Sometimes it gets so cold even the animals are hurting. That's sad.

The other day, down by the river, I saw a family out in the cold. It looked like maybe they didn't have a home. That's really, really sad. People need homes, especially in winter. I think everybody should have a house, or an apartment, or somewhere to stay warm.

My mom takes me to The Shelter when she goes to serve food to people who don't have a home. I talk with the people there.

Winger, When It's Cold
(continued)

Most of them are just like you and me, only right now they don't have a place to stay. Sometimes I take a coat and hat that I wore last year and toys that are still good, to give to a family who might be able to use them. And I get to wash down the tables when everybody's through eating. I like doing something to help out at The Shelter.

Why don't you ask your family if there's a shelter where you might take clothing or blankets for people who could use them.

Weaver Finch on Winter

Come gather round and I'll tell you a story.

Once there was an ice fairy who lived in the forest way up north. Her house was made of ice. In the morning when she wanted a drink of water, she'd build a fire in the fireplace. The ice above the fire would melt, trickling down into a glass for her to drink.

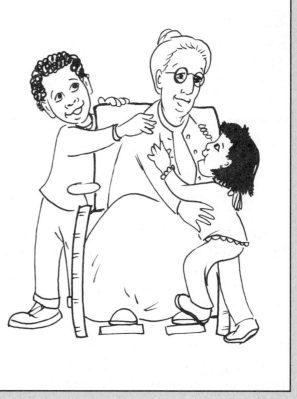

There were lots of advantages to living in an ice house. The fairy's ice cream didn't melt. She didn't need a refrigerator. And she got to ice skate any time she wanted.

What would you like about living in an ice house? _____

Finch, three, two, one. This story is done.

Death of a Family Member

Healing Wheel

 Copy a wheel like this on a piece of heavy white construction paper. Either write "Family" in the center of the wheel, or let the child glue a picture of her family at the hub.

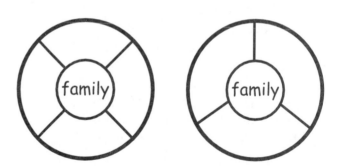

You will want to divide the wheel into as many pieces as the child has family members.

Either the child or an adult helper can cut the wheel into pieces. The child can use colored pencils or crayons to identify the pieces, "The red is me; the green is Mommy. . . ." Let the child decorate each piece as he wishes.

The pieces can be glued onto another paper that is slightly larger than the circle.

Label the pieces with names, if the child wishes.

The simple process of acknowledging family will help, even without you talking about it. Thoughts and associations about the person who has died, still belong in the circle of a family.

Skippety on Loss

I feel like I'm lost.
I have pains.
She'll never be
back here again.
I feel sick.
I am missing
her smiles and hugs
and tickly kissing.

Finger Paint

Have child choose the favorite color of the person who has died. (You might say, "Was there a color that Uncle _____ liked best?" And "If you don't know for sure, what color do you think he would've liked?") Give the child that color.

Let child finger paint. Slick, non-porous paper works best.

The process of hands smearing, smoothing, even etching in the paint, will soothe raw feelings.

Offer to add the child's favorite color.

Activity

Death

Have materials available for the children to "play" about the death. If it was through an accident, provide a car, a train, a plane, or whatever was involved. Have these corresponding items, matching as closely as possible to the circumstances of the death, out on the shelves among the other choices. You would not be instructing, or guiding, but only standing by. If the death was due to illness, a doctor's kit is a must. You might have to revamp the home corner into a "hospital" temporarily. The children may want to doctor you. That's okay. Sometimes you might join in. Other times you might not, if your presence in the play gets in the way of the children moving naturally through their own grief process. The children will "play" out their feelings. They will try to save or heal the victim. The play is the child's way of coming to terms with the loss.

You will want to refer the family to a grief support center, if you are lucky enough to have one in your area.

One caution: In early learning environments, we can't put out toy guns for the children to play with, even if it's to help a child heal from the trauma of a gun-related death. However, children will probably use their arms and hands to replicate gun shooting, or they might pick up some other toy to approximate a gun. You will have to decide yourself whether you can allow this particular therapeutic play. If you already have a school or center policy that forbids pretend shooting, this can't be allowed.

Play *can* help heal. For the sake of the child who has lost someone because of a shooting, you might let the children play "shooting" without guns if it happens naturally and as long as no one is being hurt. Keep a close watch though. If the "gun play" goes on without culminating in the perpetrator getting caught, or the victim being saved, or whatever the child sees as a satisfactory outcome, or if the child who was affected is excessively fearful, then you'll need to shift the focus to helping the child find ways to feel safe in the world. Certainly you will want to talk with your group about the circumstances and the child's loss.

Again, be sure to link the family up with a grief support center or network. There the child will be able to play act with other children who have experienced loss in the presence of a trained professional.

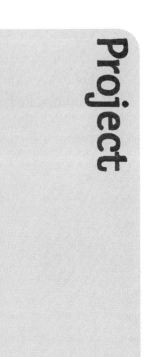

Memories

Help the child cover a shoe box. Let him decorate it as he wishes. Name it something like a Memory Box.

As things come up—thoughts, memories, items such as leaves or rocks that would've pleased the person who's died—let the child treasure away those remembrances into the box. Encourage the child to illustrate the thoughts. Add dictated words as the child shares about the item or thought.

Let the child go to the box whenever he wants. Tell him that when he is ready, he may take the box home. Don't worry if it's months before the child wants to. Children are very perceptive. They see a grieving family member. They will likely decide to protect that person from painful remembering. You'll need to cue the family member into the memory box, particularly before it goes home. Encourage the family member to go through the box with the child. Talking about the death is an essential part of healing.

Create a Memory Spot

Let the child bring in a picture of the person who has died. Be sure to include the family in your intentions. Some families will be so immersed in their own grief that any participation on your part may feel like intrusive intervention. Honor the family's wishes. Offer the involvement simply because you know how hard it will be for the parent to do these activities, because of her own grief. If an adult from the family is volunteering in the child's school or child care experience, she could carry out these activities with your backing. It may actually be preferable for you to be the child's school support though, because the child won't be trying to protect your feelings.

In an undisturbed area, set up the picture along with a vase. Together you can bring or gather things to put in the vase, in memory of the person. Other families in the group may want to informally join in the honoring, by bringing in a flower for the grieving child to add to the vase. Leave the memory spot until the child is ready to take the vase home. Let the child be involved in disassembling the memory spot.

Skippety on Sadness

My feet won't skip and play.
My grandma died today.

Winger on Death

Here's some of what I feel about people dying: It's hard. It might be the hardest thing in the world to have a close friend or family member die. At least that's how a whole lot of people feel right after someone they love dies.

And it hurts. Everything hurts for a while.

And it doesn't make much sense. I had to ask the adults in my life to help me understand what happens when people die. You can ask the adults in your life. Be sure to talk to your family if someone you know dies. Ask them to tell you what they think about death.

When I had an uncle die, I felt so sick. He was such a good friend to me. I thought I

Winger on Death
(continued)

would throw up when I heard he had died. I couldn't even move off the couch most days. I really loved my uncle.

I was scared, kinda jumpy too, for no reason.

I especially couldn't figure out how everybody in town just went along as if nothing had happened. I guess they didn't know my uncle the way I did.

My uncle helped me learn that death happens sometimes. Now I know how other people feel when someone they love dies. After awhile though, death looked different to me. I did stop hurting. Then I could think happy thoughts about my uncle. And I could remember him and talk with my family about things we did together. It's really amazing how that works. I'm so glad the hurting feelings about death don't last forever. They sure feel like they're going to at first though.

Weaver Finch on Death

Note:
Discussion here depends so much on the situation, the child, your group, the family involved. If you know a child has lost a family member, you won't want to ask questions about their tender feelings in a group setting. More than likely, the child won't be able to tell you. And that singling out may add to the isolation she will already feel. Talking with the child one-on-one, listening to her, being there for her, will give the child the support she needs. I offer Weaver Finch's story for group reading if the child in your care is already talking openly about the death.

You may overhear two children talking together about their losses. That would be a perfect opportunity to use Weaver Finch or the other characters' contributions just for the two of them. Then discussion could follow naturally, from their shared experience.

continued

Weaver Finch on Death
(continued)

Come gather round and I'll tell you a story.

Once upon a time, there was a boy who was very close to his father. They went everywhere together—to the zoo, and to the lake, fishing. But one day there was a terrible accident. The boy's father died in the accident.

The boy cried and cried. And you know what? At first his friends didn't know what to do. So they just took him tissues and they let him cry. For a long, long time, nothing really helped. At times he got mad at them, but their teacher explained he needed to be mad sometimes. That was part of being sad and missing his dad. So the friends tried to not get mad back.

One day the boy stopped crying and he started to feel like he wanted to play. He knew he could play with his friends because he could tell they cared for him. His teacher told him if he got sad and had to stop playing, his friends would understand; they wouldn't be mad at him. Sometimes that did happen. Sometimes they all played together about the accident, even when he was sad. But that was OK. That was the boy's way of getting through what happened. If he had to stop playing, he could always come back and play with his friends later. And that's just how it went, for weeks and weeks.

Finch, three, two, one. This story is only just begun. You'll have to help me know how to finish it. I do know it took a long time for things to feel hunky dory again.

Becoming Differently-Abled

Note:

You only have to read one inspiring book or see one TV special featuring a person who has become differently-abled to realize that the change need not be permanently negative. Of course, a disabling accident or illness carries with it feelings of anger and sadness. Recovery can be difficult, sometimes to the extreme. But the most moving stories come from those people who have turned what might have been a tragedy into a gift. If you care for a child who has had a life-changing accident or illness, you will want to listen to the genuine reactions of the child, including the negative. Allow acting out behavior as long as it doesn't hurt the child or others, but ultimately encourage positive thinking and forward movement.

Do remember, you are not a therapist, a physical therapist, a speech pathologist, or a counselor. When in doubt, refer families to professionals.

Note:

Be diligent in not allowing put-downs on differences.

I've substitute taught recently in a number of public schools, kindergarten through high school. I like staying in touch with a range of ages. I am troubled though by the use of one particular word at all grade levels. I've often heard "retard" in self-talk and in thoughtless put-downs of others. I usually stop the proceedings in the hallways or classrooms to talk with children about this particular put-down. I also try to do so in a way that doesn't humiliate the unknowing offender. I explain that retardation is not something to joke about, and certainly not to be used as a put-down of anyone. All children have feelings. Children who fall outside the norm, in any number of ways, especially those with obvious mental challenges, are likely very sensitive. Their feelings are no less important than those of any other children. When we identify a group of people in terms of a negative, we cause hurt to them and anyone who has a differently-abled person in his or her family or circle of friends.

You can point out that differences come in all forms. Having the way one's brain works be different from others should not be singled out any more than having large feet or a small nose. Children learn the put-down behavior. Respect is natural and can be nurtured as the norm. So can positive self-talk.

Be clear. Be firm. Simply do not allow such references in your school or learning environment. Writing this passage has reminded me to be braver still, to talk with other adults to form an education coalition that would make using the word completely unacceptable. In fact, in the months that this book has been in process, I have been more diligent. The word "retard" has pretty much dropped from our schools' colloquialisms. I hope it's been replaced with acceptance and understanding.

Imaginative Play

Therapeutic Reenactment

Imaginative play will always help both the child affected by the change and the children in the group.

Use doll house and small dolls.

Children can fashion crutches out of pipe cleaners.

Small boxes can be cut into a wheelchair. Make wheels out of cardboard. Affix with brads.

Children can help larger, movable dolls relearn walking, or go through physical therapy, if that is part of the child's experience.

Borrow child-size crutches. Let children take turns attempting to walk using only one leg.

Blindfolds, the fold-up cane, and ETA's (electronic travel aids) can be used or simulated, allowing the children to empathize in earnest with people who have lost their sight.

Simple sign language can be taught to the group, if a child or child's sibling loses hearing. Don't hesitate to call on a volunteer if you aren't versed in sign language yourself.

Differently-Abled Gingerbread Girls and Boys

Roll out gingerbread cookie dough.

Let your helper or volunteer make the cookies, only altering, with cookies missing a part of their body.

If you have a child or a child's family member lose a leg or arm, you could eliminate that limb from all of the cookies. Bake.

Be sure *an adult* puts the cookie sheets in and out of the oven. Frost the cooled cookies, if desired.

A variation: Each cookie could be missing one part—an arm, a foot, the eyes, the mouth—making all cookies different. Each cookie is special. Each cookie is different.

Use the cookies as follow-up to discussions about how all people are different. Not all of us have sight in both eyes, the use of our arms, etc. We are all gifted and talented in numerous ways. We are all special.

Weaver Finch on Dealing with Being Differently-Abled

Come gather round and I'll tell you a story.

Once there was an old woman. It was the first day that the woman got her wheelchair. Yes, you're right. That woman was me.

I remember how happy I was, because having my wheelchair meant I could get out of bed and get around on my own. I don't know if I've ever told you. I'm not able to walk anymore. Maybe you guessed it. My wheelchair makes it so I can go almost anywhere.

When I started going out I noticed how children would stare at the wheelchair, trying to figure out how the wheel worked. Besides which, grown-ups seemed to not know what to do; sometimes they tried to not even look at me. That made me sad. I wanted people to see me as me, only just a little different than I'd always been. I didn't mind too much, because I'm an older person and am happy to be able to get around at all. I thought a lot about children after that though, children who use a wheelchair. I wondered how they feel when people stare at them or avoid them altogether.

As soon as I could, I started going to a rehabilitation center to volunteer with the children who were in wheelchairs. And I found they felt the same way I did. Sure they'd like to be able to walk. And sometimes it made them mad that they couldn't. But most of the time they felt like any other person. They just got around in a different way, that's all.

We're all different, in one way or another. Some of us are tall, some short. Some of us see better than others. Some run faster or jump higher. Some are quick on the keyboard. We're all different, in one way or 'nother. I'm glad. Seems to me that's what makes each of us so special.

Finch, three, two, one. This story is done.

Divorce

Playdough

There are many recipes for playdough. Here's one that's simple, surefire, and requires no cooking. Store in seal-tight plastic containers in between uses.

Let the child help make the dough with you or an adult volunteer.

Mix the following ingredients together in a large bowl:

2 cups flour
2 Tbsp. cornstarch
1 cup salt
1 Tbsp. vegetable oil
1+ cup warm water
food coloring

The child who's in the middle of divorce will likely alternate between pounding and nest-making uses of the playdough, probably with great feeling.

Project

Feeling Textures

Present the child undergoing divorce with a "feeling" box and lid that lifts off.

Offer scraps of materials with different textures, such as cloth, in velvet, rayon, flannel, corduroy, etc.

sandpaper

papers with different feels

nonporous cardboard or vinyl

Let the child pick different pieces to glue onto pieces of paper, just smaller than the size of the box.

You might go through the papers, such as one with especially soft fabric glued on it, asking "Does this remind you of something?" If the child has an association, write it down on the back of the paper.

The child puts the papers into the box. You can sort through the box together, reading the notes, and adding to the feelings from time to time. The association might come in words like "rocking by the fire," rather than a statement of feeling. Be sure to accept the child's response, whatever it is.

Activity

Pounding Stump

a large block of wood, or section of tree stump, without knots

large-headed nails

child-size hammer

Children take turns pounding. Designate a line behind which those waiting must stand so that no one gets hit. Always be sure such activities are supervised by an adult. The pounding works best if the wood has wide grain, and the nails aren't too long.

The simple act of a pounding motion will help move angry feelings through a child, in a positive, acceptable activity.

Squooshy Sculpting

Children rip up cardboard egg cartons into little pieces.

Have them soak the pieces in a bowl of warm water, overnight.

The next day, drain off the excess water.

Children can use this mixture to mold, build, sculpt, slap, splat, goosh. If it dries out, or the children want to use it a second or third day, reconstitute with a little warm water. Any final products can be set on wax paper to dry.

Optional: Paint the sculptures with poster paint. However, the process is much more important than the product. There need not be a product for this activity to produce results in soothed feelings and calmed behavior.

Bananas in Crumbs

Here's a positive use for bottled up anger:

Have the child who's going through divorce crush crackers into crumbs. Put down a layer of waxed paper, then crackers, then another layer of waxed paper. The child can pound with his fist.

Have the child roll 1-inch-wide banana slices, so the edges are covered in crumbs.

Family Carryalls

Help the child make two carrying cases. A decorated cereal box, or a bank check box will do. Attach cardboard handles.

Help the child cut out standard family figures smaller than the size of the box you've chosen. The figures should match her two new families, even if the figures are just Mom in one and Dad in the other. Include a figure of the child.

Let the child put the cut-outs in the two separate carryalls. The child can use the figures to express feelings about the family's new order. Remember, the "expression" may come in angry behavior rather than words.

Don't direct the child, other than to offer the project, describing the carryalls as two places for your family now. If the child is unable to accept the divorce, she may want the family members all in one case. Or any step-family members may be discarded altogether. Or the child may need two cut-outs of himself, showing the unwillingness to appear to be choosing between the parents. The purpose of the project is to allow the child to give words, or alternately silent actions, to her feelings. Resist directing those feelings.

Eventually, the child may move his own figure from one carryall to the other as visitations progress. In any case, this project is a way for the child to be in control, and to be working through her feelings.

Winger on Divorce

I don't like divorce. I think it's hard on the children. Grown-ups say some divorces make life better. Maybe they do, but divorce still hurts.

I was really, really mad when my mom and dad got a divorce. That's for sure.

I'll tell you how it was for me. My stomach felt like somebody was squeezing it. My neck felt pinched between my shoulders. My eyes started twitching. That was because I got tired of crying all the time.

I started to feel better when I told people how I felt. I told my parents to please not fight anymore. That was making me so scared all the time. You know what? They actually listened and stopped yelling in front of me. That helped a lot! If your parents get divorced, just be sure to talk to them or talk to another adult you feel close to about your feelings. Be sure to tell people what you need. It's okay to say, "I need a big hug." Or "I need to know it wasn't my fault." I can tell you the answer to that: Divorces are never the kids' fault.

Weaver Finch on Divorce

Note:
As with death, you will probably want to read and talk privately with the one child, rather than sharing this with a group. If you're just talking with the child who is going through a divorce, you can ask the child what it's like for her. That way you retain control over the confidentiality of the information the child might share. Do not encourage children to divulge personal family information in a group setting.

Come gather round and I'll tell you a story.

I'll tell you a story about when I was little. For days and days my parents were fighting. Longer than that. Weeks and weeks, maybe years and years. Then one night my father hit my mother. And then he left. I saw it happen. I wanted to run to him. I knew he was sorry. But he'd slammed the door so hard, it seemed impossible to open it again.

But there was Mother, sitting all slumped over. I went to her and put my arm around her. I patted her and patted her while she cried. Finally Mother reached out and gathered me on her lap. She patted and patted me.

That's what happened to me when I was little.

I did get to see my father again. He called and they set up a time for us to get together. It took weeks more to work things out. My parents did get divorced. That meant they weren't going to live together and they weren't going to be married anymore.

Some people who yell, or even hit, can learn how to stop. Sometimes it's the mother who has to do the learning about how to work out disagreements in a caring way. Sometimes the parents end up staying together, but sometimes they do get divorced.

When I did finally get to see my father, that was called visitation. My parents worked out the visitations so that I could still have a mother and a father. Each family whose parents get divorced has a different story though. I know it doesn't always work out for children to be able to keep both parents. That's the hardest part about divorce.

Finch, three, two, one. This story is done.

Drug and Alcohol Abuse

Note:

It is not within the scope of this activity book to attempt to assist you in determining drug and alcohol abuse. When a teacher has documented and sincere reason to suspect abuse and neglect though, he is obligated to report the evidence or behaviors to the Child Protective Services. Because of the delicate nature of handling such cases, and the potential for increased harm to the child, the teachers and caregivers need to relinquish responsibility to full-time CPS workers. In-depth investigation should be carried out (and insisted on).

The teacher will serve the child by providing a neutral, safe place at the child's school or child care center. If the parent feels judgment or antagonism from the teacher, the parent is likely to withdraw the child. The teacher or caregiver should take care not to jeopardize the child's opportunity for this stability.

Imaginative Play

A Safe and Loving Home

Within a traditional home-corner setting, the child will work on family interactions through playing with the other children. As teacher, you can record observations, but be careful not to prompt the child's behavior. With a phone in the home corner, the child may rehearse dialing 911. This would be one of the behaviors you would want to record. But certainly, taken alone, it would not be an indication of a problem at home. A child might have seen the morning news, for instance, where a preschooler saved a family member by dialing 911. She might be testing out her abilities to do the same. Being available, listening carefully to the children's words and actions, will help you determine the meanings behind their play. When you need to understand something, try giving a simple statement, such as, "I heard you dialing 911." Allow the child to respond with more information. You may ask directly, but you want to be sure not to put words or ideas into the child's mouth.

Have home-corner equipment available, including:

babies and toddler dolls

care-giving items: bottles, blankets, clothes, baby food

play telephone

Children may want to play-act baby care if they are feeling particularly needy.

Activity

Soothing Selves

You will also serve the child by encouraging participation in other soothing activities, such as:

warm water play

playdough

sand play

flannel board story pieces (See Appendix for more information about how these can be used.)

Fire

Putting out Fire in Water Table

small play house and family figures
fire truck, or truck that you can tape a fire department sign onto
paper smoke curls
water in small spray bottle
plastic tubing for hoses
bed (a block will do) and bedding (out of material scrap or paper)

A Safe Meeting Spot

Show the children your safe outdoor meeting spot if there should be a fire.

If you don't already carry out fire drills, you must. Tell the children before you carry out the first drill. Be sure to practice getting out of the building and gathering at your safe spot. Repeat regularly. This will give the child who has been through a fire, a sense of much-needed security.

Encourage children to talk with their families about their safe meeting spots at home.

Fire's Out Crackers

Have the fire-affected child help with snack.
Top crackers with a slice of sweet red pepper.
Let the child spray on creamy cheese topping to "put out the fire."

Skippety on Fires

Dawny smelled the smoke,
oh, choke.
She dropped onto the floor.
The flames were loud.
The doorknob hot.
She couldn't get out the door.

Dawny smelled the smoke,
oh, choke.
She crawled to the nearest window.
Out and down
she jumped, ker ugh!
"I think I broke my toe!"

Dawny smelled the smoke,
oh, choke.
She limped to her neighbor's yard.
"Call the fire department!
Call 911!"
Dawny yelled and yelled real hard.

Dawny smelled the smoke,
oh choke.
The flames flickered away.
The firefighters
put it out.
Everyone was okay.

For weeks and weeks, Dawny cringed.
She thought she still smelled smoke.
And everywhere
she went she said,
"Fire is no joke!"

Winger on Fires

Here's what I remember about fires. Once I was in my room, coloring a picture. I was waiting for dinner. I thought I smelled smoke. But Mom's always burning something when she cooks, so I kept on coloring. Then I heard the smoke alarm go off. Mom's always fanning that alarm to get it to stop when she burns something, so I went on coloring. But the alarm didn't stop. So I skoochied over to my door. I felt the door. It was cold, so I knew it was okay to open it, just a teeny little bit. But a whole bunch of smoke sucked right in my face. I slammed my door! I was so scared I almost forgot what to do. But then I yelled and screamed. And while I was yelling, I got my window unlocked. I was already on top of my desk, so I held onto the window ledge, leaned out the window and lowered myself down onto the ground. It wasn't very far.

Then I ran to the poplar tree where we're supposed to meet if there's ever a fire. I was even more scared when I didn't see Mom, but I stayed right there like we'd practiced. In a minute, she came running around from the back of the house. And then the fire engines came up the street with their lights flashing and their siren screaming. Mom had been out in the garden when our dinner caught on fire. The firefighters put out the flames, which were just in the kitchen.

That fire wasn't any fun. Mom and I learned a lesson though. Now we know, if ever the smoke alarm goes off, we take it seriously. I'm sure glad we had a family plan so I knew what to do. Do you have a plan in case there's ever a fire at your place?

Friend or Sibling Goodbye

Note:
While children are impacted by a close friend or family member moving to a new town or situation, they can also become anxious and sad about the changes inherent in a school or child care center closing. Broaden the activities in a Friend or Sibling Goodbye, to help the child give words to feelings about school farewells. Remember, many children will not be able to articulate feelings, so listen to their actions as well as their words.

Activity

Keeping in Touch

With the child, fill out a stamped post card with her home address. If the child is able, have her write her own name.

Let the child put the post card in an envelope to give to the departing friend or sibling.

By using the home address, you involve the child's family in the process of keeping in touch. Encourage the child to bring in the post card note from the friend to share with the class.

Going Away Present

Allow the child to make a present for the departing friend or sibling.

Talk with the child about what was special about having that person nearby. Write down the response.

Give the child a piece of paper on which to illustrate his words.

Tape the words of explanation at the bottom.

Frame the picture by cutting a border of construction paper to place over the picture, so that the picture and words show.

If the child has more energy for the project, offer materials for decorating the border.

Provide a large envelope or box in which the child can take the present to the departing friend or sibling.

"Thinking-of-You" Box

Offer the child a small box for keeping thoughts about the person who's going away.

Together, decide where to put the box for easy access and safe-keeping.

Provide small pieces of paper in a little stack next to the box.

For a week or a month (whatever seems necessary), let the child bring slips of paper to you, so he can dictate messages, thoughts of, remembrances (such as "I liked it when. . . ."").

The child colors or adds to the note, then slips it in the box.

At some point, the child will reach completion. She will no longer need to record her feelings as she will have felt heard in the loss.

Ask the child if he wants help mailing the box to the person. Or he may want to keep the box for himself to look through when he's older. The child will know what's right for him.

Winger on Being Left

Here's what I said when my brother moved away to the police academy:

"This is disasterdly! My big brother has always been here. I mean, I grew up with him. When I was born, he was here. When I was a little kid, he was here. Now I'm starting in school and where will my brother be? He'll be at college. This is disasterdly! (That's what I said.) What will I do without him here?"

Now, I've lived quite awhile without my brother nearby. It's gotten easier. We have kept in touch. He and I do special things together when he comes home. I have done okay without my brother living at home.

Did you ever know anyone who went away?

Weaver Finch on Letting Go

Come gather round and I'll tell you a story.

I think one of the hardest things in life is letting someone go.

You know, once there was a woman. She had gotten sick and after a lot of medicines and doctors' help, the woman realized she wasn't going to be able to walk again.

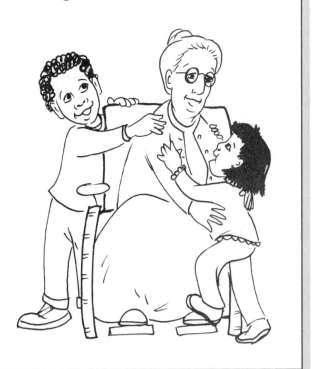

Her grown-up daughter came home to see her. They had such a good time. They talked, they read books out loud, and they looked through old photographs. The daughter helped the woman pick out a wheelchair. Then they went together to the park and another day they went to a

Weaver Finch on Letting Go
(continued)

friend's house. It was hard for the woman to maneuver the wheelchair, so her daughter helped her at first.

But one day the daughter had to leave, to go back to the town where she lived and worked. On the going-away day, the woman and her daughter cried and laughed and cried some more. They were happy about their time together. They were sad it was ending.

The daughter gathered up her things and went out to her car. The woman followed in her wheelchair. They stopped on the front walk. The daughter hugged the woman, a big hug to last a long time. Then she got in her car. They waved goodbye and the daughter left.

On the first afternoon, the old woman couldn't stop thinking about the daughter. She missed her so much.

The next day the woman thought of her daughter all morning, so she wheeled out in her garden, and wrote a letter to put out for the mail carrier.

The next day the woman's friends stopped by. They stayed for lunch and into the afternoon, so the woman _____. (When do you think she thought of her daughter that day?)

The next day she got a letter from her daughter.

The woman and her daughter kept in touch. They kept writing and sometimes they called. For the woman's birthday, the daughter gave her a computer and taught her how to use it. Then the woman and her grown daughter e-mailed each other nearly every day. And the daughter visited as often as she could.

Finch, three, two, one. This story is done.

Parent's Hospital Stay

Note:
Since a parent's hospital stay impacts the child most, I've put adjusting to hospitals in that context. Adapt activities for a sibling or grandparent having to stay in the hospital. You may also have a child himself needing to be hospitalized. In that case you can involve the other children in the school or child care setting, and offer activities before and after for the child herself.

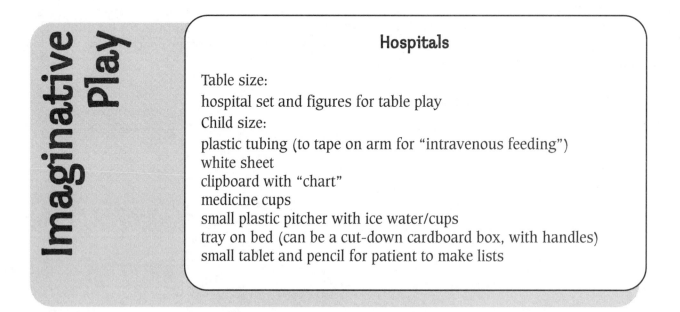

Imaginative Play

Hospitals

Table size:
hospital set and figures for table play
Child size:
plastic tubing (to tape on arm for "intravenous feeding")
white sheet
clipboard with "chart"
medicine cups
small plastic pitcher with ice water/cups
tray on bed (can be a cut-down cardboard box, with handles)
small tablet and pencil for patient to make lists

"Here's What I'm Doing While You're In The Hospital" Book

Using one of your premade books, let the child dictate school activities.

The child will illustrate the pages.

Work on the book for a few days or a week, then let the child take or send it to the parent in the hospital.

Picture Box

Have the child help you wrap the top and the bottom pieces of a tiny jewelry box in shiny paper.

Talk to someone in the family about getting a picture of the family's patient, to cut and put in the box.

The box then becomes a treasure. When the child has to go from relatives, to babysitter, to hospital as inevitably happens in the upheaval accompanying a drastic change in routine, the child can tuck the box in a coat pocket or backpack. It especially helps to have the picture box to take to bed when the child is missing the hospitalized family member.

Winger on Poppa's Hospital Stay

Here's what I remember about hospitals from when my Poppa still lived with us. When he had to go into the hospital, I felt sick myself. I thought I was going to throw up. Only I didn't have the flu or anything.

When we went to see him, Poppa talked funny. Mom said it was because of the medicine he was taking. It made me feel icky, though, for him to be sounding all mumbly. He didn't even laugh right.

In the hallway I heard my mom talking about the "operation," but when I asked her what that meant, she just said everything's going to be fine. I wanted to know what was going to happen.

Some days I didn't want to go see him. I just wanted to stay home and watch cartoons. Even though I missed Poppa so much, it was weird. I didn't want to think about him. Cartoons help with not thinking, don't they? Some days a babysitter stayed at home with me, so Mom could visit as long as she wanted at the hospital.

When I did go, I usually felt better afterwards. And Poppa seemed to feel better too.

Finally Poppa got to come home. They took him down the hallway in a wheelchair. The wheelchair was just like Weaver Finch's. Poppa said he wanted to walk, but the nurse said it was the rules. They had to wheel him all the way out to the car.

It turned out though that Poppa had to use the wheelchair at home too, for several more days. He told me if I'd get my wheelchair license, I could drive. It felt good to be laughing with Poppa again.

Weaver Finch on Moms or Dads in the Hospital

Come gather round and I'll tell you a story.

Once when I was very little my mother had to be in the hospital. At first I stayed with my aunt. Then I stayed with my grandma and grandpa.

A friend of ours knew I'd miss my mother since I was so young. So before Mother's operation our friend brought over a big box with a whole bunch of smaller boxes inside. Each little present was wrapped in a different pretty paper. Mother's friend said that there was a present in the big box for every day that Mother was in the hospital. Only the presents were for me! She said the presents might help me get through the missing-Mother days. If I opened one present every day, then when there was only one present left, I'd know Mother would be home the very next day. That would be the best present of all.

Every day someone in the family took me to the hospital to visit Mother. We'd go up in an elevator, then walk down the long, long halls. Finally they'd stop at a doorway and I could see Mother in a high-up bed.

Every day I took my new present to show Mother. Some days I let her keep it, and some days I took it home to play with.

On the first day the wrapping was _____(color) with little _____ (unicorns, puppies, or whatever the children choose) all over it. What do you suppose was in that first box? _____ (Let the children guess, beginning with the child whose parent is in the hospital. (Repeat, until interest lags; that can be the final day.) That's the way the wrapping and the boxes went. All pretty. All different. All fun. But the most fun was when Mother came home again.

Finch, three, two, one. This story is done.

Moving

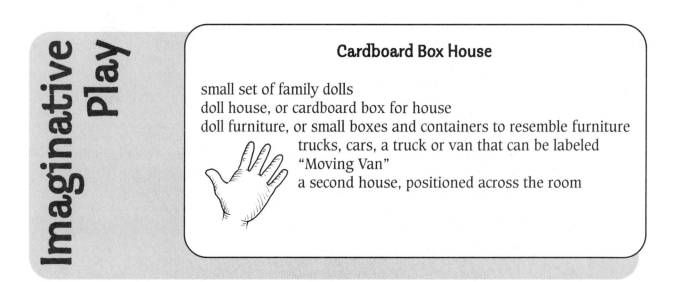

Imaginative Play

Cardboard Box House

small set of family dolls
doll house, or cardboard box for house
doll furniture, or small boxes and containers to resemble furniture
trucks, cars, a truck or van that can be labeled "Moving Van"
a second house, positioned across the room

Goodbye Box

If the child is moving out of the area, assign two boxes, about the size of a shoe box, for "Goodbye Boxes."

The child who's moving may use one of the boxes to hold pictures, with dictated notes, or to hold special rocks or other objects gathered as farewell remembrances for everyone in the group.

The other box is for the group to gather remembrances or thoughts for the child who's moving, such as an acorn from Jill or the title of an often-read book from Ben.

You can give suggestions such as these to establish that the offerings don't have to be elaborate or complicated. You also want to be sure the children know not to give away things that belong to everyone, such as parts of a building set.

When the goodbye day arrives, the boxes are exchanged, forming a bit of closure to the time together.

Remember Book

Help the child assemble a remembrance book.

As you turn through the book, the left page will be about the old house, the right, the new. Here are some ideas for the pages:

old sounds	new sounds
old smells	new smells
old hiding places	new hiding places
old neighbors	new neighbors

If the child is moving out of your area, she can finish the book with a grown-up in the new house. Be sure to show a family member the design.

Skippety on Moving

If we're moving,
where will I sleep?
Where will I put
the rocks I keep?
Where will our table go?
Where will the chairs?
Will there be trees outside?
Will there be bears?

Skippety Again, Remembering Moves

First there was the Fly House,
then the Apple Pie House.
Then there was the Little House
down by the Slough.
Then there was the Town House.
Then that big old Brown House.
Then there was the Willow House
where we got the flu.

Then there was the house
with the caterpillars everywhere.
Oh, and the house with
the slugs, slugs, slugs.
Then there was the Green House
and the Inbetween House
and then there was the house
where the neighbors all did drugs.

Skippety Again, Remembering Moves
(continued)

Remember the Squirrel House?
Then the Windy
Whirl House.
Then there was the house
where the landlord gave us hugs. YUK!
I want to come upon
a stay-put resting house
a quiet little nesting house
that we can call Home.

Winger on Moving

Here's what I think about moving:
I didn't think I would like moving at all. We had always lived in our old apartment. I knew where I was when I woke up in the night. I knew the kids in my neighborhood. And I liked visiting the lady next door.

Then when we moved I wondered where all my stuff would be. It took me a long time to unpack everything. And Mom had to help me learn where it was safe to go in our new neighborhood. After awhile though, I got used to our new place. It turned out there were fun things about both our old apartment and our new one.

I do remember when we moved, I took my blanky and my Buddy doll with me in the car. I had to. Just in case I might need them in a hurry in our new place.

Weaver Finch on Moving

Come gather round and I'll tell you a story.

One of the hardest things about my growing up was the moving. My family moved every year or two. It seemed I never got to settle into a place, or make close friends. Of course that was a long time ago.

I had an aunt who lived with us for a number of years. She would play this game with me to make the moving easier.

My auntie would say, "When I packed up all my things, I found a baby spoon that I didn't know I still had." Then it would be my turn, "When I packed up all my things, I found a _____ that I didn't know I still had."

(Repeat around your group, giving each child a chance to think of a lost item.)

By the time my auntie and I were through with the game, I was through with feeling sad about moving.

Finch, three, two, one. This story is done.

Birth or Acquisition of a Pet

Note:
Young children will consider a new family pet a big event. This section is not meant to encourage pet ownership for young children. Generally preschoolers can't be expected to assume sole care of pets. Often classrooms have pets that can substitute nicely for home pet ownership. Learning pet care in an educational setting can develop into responsible pet ownership in subsequent years. While this section acknowledges the birth of pets, it is certainly not intended as support for pet breeding.

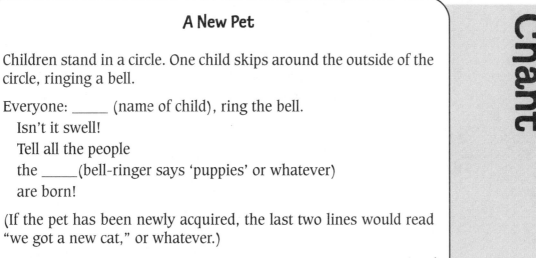

A New Pet

Children stand in a circle. One child skips around the outside of the circle, ringing a bell.

Everyone: _____ (name of child), ring the bell.
  Isn't it swell!
  Tell all the people
  the _____ (bell-ringer says 'puppies' or whatever)
  are born!

(If the pet has been newly acquired, the last two lines would read "we got a new cat," or whatever.)

continued

Action Chant

A New Pet
(continued)

If your group has gotten a new pet, let all the children take turns ringing the bell. If you have a child whose family has recently acquired a pet, let that child be the bell-ringer. Repeat with new bell-ringer and new pet, if applicable.

Variation: Groups of older children can make this more interesting by having the (first) child stand outside the circle. Have the children in the circle begin skipping in one direction. Once the circle is moving nicely, have the child skip in the opposite direction. Begin the song. When the song comes to an end, all the children stop. The ringer then passes the bell to the child next to him. That child moves outside the circle. Repeat.

Celebrative Dance

Let children put a handful of small rocks in yogurt containers. Tape shut.

A rhythmic dance can turn from a positive to a negative experience very quickly. Be prepared to lead the children with preventive suggestions such as these. While shaking the containers . . .

hop on one foot
shake over your head
shake behind your back
shake as loud as you can
shake as quietly as you can

ripple the shakes throughout the room, that is, when you point to one section, they shake, then stop as you point to the next, or have ripples build as the whole group shakes faster and faster shake while sitting down

Permanent Shaker Set

You can make a permanent set of shakers of varying sounds, by putting sand, pea gravel, broken twigs, etc. in containers. Tape lids on. Cover with construction paper or even strips from paper bags. Decorate with crayons, markers, glued-on rick rack, what-have-you that won't rub or shake off.

Mama and Babies

celery sticks with peanut butter
Let snack helper place in the peanut butter: one grape and a row of baby raisins, or one chunk of pea pod and a row of frozen peas.

Take Home Gift Idea for the Mother Pet

Mobile to hang above pets' bed:
Let the children make a mobile out of any materials designed to relate to the mother and babies. You might offer magazines to cut out, pipe cleaners to twist into shapes, or cardboard cut-outs to decorate.

 When you assemble the mobile pieces, go for simple balance.

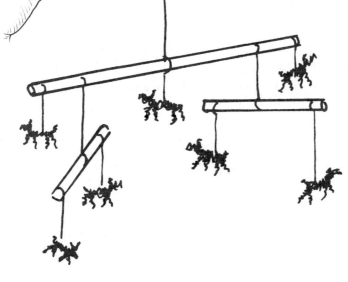

Cotton Ball Babies

Let child prepare a little pet bed, perhaps with shredded paper in a berry container, or in a folded-paper container.

Snip straw in 1- to 2-inch lengths.

Child glues a cotton ball on the end of each straw.

Eyes can be dotted on the balls with pointed-tip markers.

Triangles of felt or paper can be glued on for ears, if desired.

Child pokes the straws into the bedding, as if their pet babies have gone to bed.

Alternately, let the child use the materials to create his own design for the baby animals.

Weaver Finch on Pets

Come gather round and I'll tell you a story.

You know children, when I was little, I had a calico cat. When my cat was little, she used to climb up a tree trunk just outside the front door. She'd claw her way up a few feet, then fall back down, tumble, tumble. That's how she got her name.

Because of my auntie's allergies, Tumble wasn't allowed in the house. I don't know how she got in that one night. I didn't let her in. But somehow she squeaked through an open door or pushed her way through an open window. I didn't even know she was inside!

I woke up to little peeping, sucking sounds (smack lips). I looked down on the bottom of my bed. There was Tumble, licking and kissing three little kittens. They were nursing, with their eyes tightly closed. I remember thinking how lucky I was that Tumble gave birth on my bed. I named the kittens right then: the orange one, Morning, the gray one, Beddy, and the little calico kitten, Quilt. I got out of bed very slowly so as not to disturb Tumble's babies, then I skittered down the hall to tell the rest of the family.

Mother hadn't realized Tumble was ready to be a momma. As soon as possible, she took Tumble to the vet to get her spayed. That was OK. I knew we needed to be sure she didn't have lots of kittens, but I sure enjoyed the one litter born on my bed.

Finch, three, two, one. This story is done.

Parent's Remarriage

Note:
Marriage will mean different things to different families. To some it means a new family configuration, to others it means a public acknowledgement of an already established living unit. It's important to not make assumptions or judgments. Use only the activities that match the child's situation.

Project

Shadow Boxes

Using playdough or soft clay, let children make figures (can be merely blobs in various sizes) of what the family will look like after the new marriage.

Let the child help you make a shadow-box out of a cereal box.

The child can place the figures in the box, for display.

Variation: For some children, it may be more important to acknowledge both the old and new families. Show the child a way to make two sides in the shadow box by putting a cardboard partition in between. One would show figures depicting the original family, another would show the family after remarriage.

Celebrate Anew

Cut bread in circles.

Using a mixture of peanut butter and honey, let child frost the circles of bread.

Cut banana in candle-like pieces. Let child stand a "candle" up in each piece of bread. Poke a piece of coconut in the top for a wick.

Pretend Cake

Set a recyclable plastic cake cover on a round of cardboard.

Either let the child glue crumpled tissue paper all over the cover, for frosting, or use soap flakes and food coloring, whipped together, to spread on the cake cover.

Show the child how to fold and twist pipe cleaners for pretend candles.

Wedding

When completely dry, let the child use the cake in imaginative play for a wedding celebration.

Activity

Celebration with Rhythm Blocks

Let the child help you pound strap handles on wooden block pieces (not those from your block set).

Have all the children decorate the handle side of their blocks, two for each. (You may want to save these as a set for use throughout the year for other celebrative events.)

Before the actual wedding, the child can make a wedding announcement during circle or group time. If the child is shy about speaking in the group, you and he may want to make a sign that he holds for you to read.

Then the child chooses a marching song from your music collection. The child leads the group around the room (or follows your lead), with everyone either pounding or shuffling their rhythm blocks.

Project

Families

Pound a nail hole in a frozen juice lid, close to the edge. Turn the lid over. Let the child pound to flatten the back of the hole.

Help the child make teeny cut-outs of family members—two sets, one of the parts of the first family, and another set of the entire family after remarriage.

Again, these can be outlines or merely scraps with faces. Help the child paste these, one set on each side of the lid.

Let the child pick a color of yarn. Thread a piece of yarn about 14-inches long through the hole, and tie it at the ends.

The child may hang this on a cubby hook, or even wear it. This may open the avenue to one-on-one discussions about the changes. A simple observation, "You have your family as it used to be hanging up," might elicit a verbal response. As in other changes, be sure not to put words in the child's mouth. She will no doubt use body language and actions to express her feelings as much as words.

Winger on Remarriage

Can I talk to you about something? It's something I'm kind of worried about. My poppa has been telling me for a long time that he's going to get married again.

Now my mom says it's true. He really is. And I have to go to the wedding. Has this happened to any of you? _____ What was it like? _____

If my Poppa's new wife has kids, does that make us related? Actually, she does have two little boys.

Since they'll have a bigger family than just my mom, my little sister and me, will I have to move there? I don't want to leave my mom. And if those little boys are going to be there with my dad, it's going to change our TV nights. I don't know what time with my dad will be like now.

Did you have worries like this before one of your parents got remarried? _____

Thank you. It helps to know I'm not the only one who's gone through a parent remarrying. It seems like I'd better talk to my dad some more, so that I'll really know what's going on.

Home Repair or Remodeling

Remodeling a House

Let children build a home, Lincoln Log style using short lengths of two-by-fours, just a couple of layers tall.

Children can step into their home.

Offer suggestions such as:

pretend kitchen—cooking dandelions on a flat rock
pretend living room—playing tic tac toe in the dirt

If you play along with them at first, they'll soon get the idea that this can be inventive play, without the need for elaborate props.

When it's time to remodel, everyone has to move out, and the walls are changed in size or shape. The disruption of real remodeling gets to be played out. Consult the child whose family is undergoing the upheaval themselves for process specifics that can be brought into play.

House Building

Use prepared biscuit dough:

Give each child two pieces.

The children cut each of their biscuits in four pieces.

They roll their pieces into boards.

Lincoln log style, the children can build a small house onto greased cookie sheets.

Bake four minutes longer than for regular biscuits. Be sure *an adult* puts the cookie sheets in and out of the oven.

When cool, the house can be roofed with a slice of cheese, or eaten plain, with milk.

Popsicle Houses

Using popsicle sticks, the children can build small houses.

Roof with a folded stiff paper. Adept project-makers can even glue rows of small paper on to the folded roof, for shingles.

They can glue on paper windows and doors.

The children can each make their own remodeling changes in window size or style, with decks added, etc.

Remodeling Doll's House

Help the child make a doll house out of a cardboard box. Make doors and windows by cutting where the child tells you.

Then let the child color the house.

The child may want to roof the house using paper squares.

When the house is done, let the child play, using small doll house figures.

Then give the child an opportunity to remodel.

continued

Project

Remodeling Doll's House
(continued)

The child can make choices and changes, such as:

new roof
larger windows
different door
new siding

The play with the doll house figures can go on during the remodeling, giving the child a chance to voice her family's frustrations with real-life remodeling through the doll's voices.

If a child's family has been involved in a several-month remodeling, he will have lots to contribute regarding stresses on the home environment.

Skippety on Home Repairs

Bam! Bam!
Thunk. Thunk.
Bam! Bam!
Thunk. Thunk.
Scritch, scuffer,
scritch, scruffer,
Bam! Bam! Bam!

Rruhm a rruhm a rruhm, puh!
Tat tat, tat tat.
Rruhm a rruhm a rruhm, puh!
Tat tat, tat, tat.

Rreehm a rreehm a rreehm a
Tat tat tat.
Thunk, thunk, scritch.
Bam! Bam! Bam!

Box House Remodel

Query your parents. Who among them are in the building trades?

Who has ends of pvc pipes and screw-on fittings?

Who has tile?

What about wood scraps?

Double check safety of materials, before they are donated. Make sure they have no adhesives, or other chemical compound residues.

Do not include any wiring, even in pretend play. You don't *want* children working with wiring on their own later.

Provide a large cardboard box for the children to "remodel."

Remember the process matters more than the product. Focus on allowing the children to create, inventing their own solutions to remodeling dilemmas.

Offer poster paint for their finishing touches.

Winger on Remodeling

I know a little bit about remodeling. When Mom decided to put in a new shower, we did the tear-out ourselves, Mom and me.

First, Mom said an adult always needs to turn off the electricity before starting to work. So she did. Then we put on masks so we wouldn't breathe in any harmful dust. My mom believes in safety first.

Next we took our hammers and bam, bam, bammed on the bathroom wall. Do you know what a crow bar is? We used a crow bar to pull and pull all the wall boards off. We don't have any plaster or any lead paint in our bathroom; that's why I could help too. In some places Mom used a hand saw to get the boards to break off straight. It took us a long time to get all the walls pulled out. But we did it.

continued

Winger on Remodeling
(continued)

We had to carry boxes of chunked up boards down the hallway and out the front door. It was lots of work, but I didn't mind. I helped carry every box!

Then the plumbers came with the new, bigger shower and tub to put in where the old wall had been. And we put a big cupboard where the shower used to be. Mom let me paint the cupboard myself, while a friend from up the street helped her put in the tile. (You know, tiles are those smooth squares that it's okay for the water to get on all the time.) Mom and her friend put up the tile in colored zigzag patterns.

The bathroom's pretty now. Shiny and bright. I liked helping Mom with the remodeling.

Weaver Finch on Remodeling

Come gather round and I'll tell you a story.

I have a friend. Once, quite a while ago, my friend got the idea to change some things in his stick-built house. First he wanted to make it easier for me to come visit, so he bang, bang, banged up a ramp to his front door. But the door wasn't wide enough for the wheelchair ramp, so he rip, bang, bang rip bang banged. He tore out the old doorway and put in a much sturdier, wide door.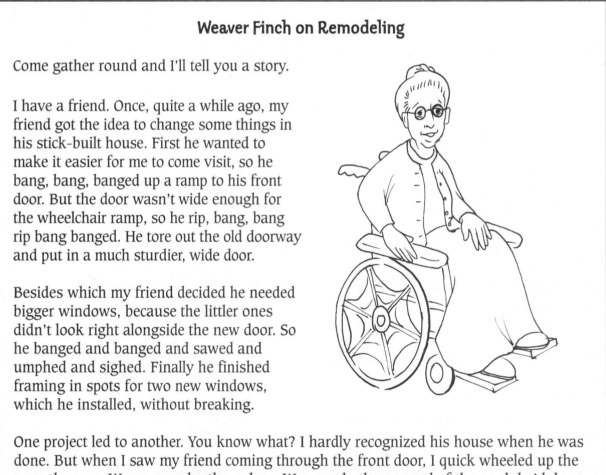

Besides which my friend decided he needed bigger windows, because the littler ones didn't look right alongside the new door. So he banged and banged and sawed and umphed and sighed. Finally he finished framing in spots for two new windows, which he installed, without breaking.

One project led to another. You know what? I hardly recognized his house when he was done. But when I saw my friend coming through the front door, I quick wheeled up the smooth ramp. We gave each other a hug. We were both so proud of the work he'd done. But before I let him show me the rest, I turned my wheelchair around, and went wheee down the ramp, just for fun!

Finch, three, two, one. This story is done.

Change in Teacher or Caregiver

Note:

In some schools or child care centers, a custodian or special volunteer plays a significant role in the children's lives. Perhaps the cook knows every child by name and enjoys daily conversations. You can use activities here to acknowledge special relationships with any adults who might be leaving. Closure helps children and adults.

Closure with the Teacher Who's Leaving

To celebrate your time spent together, work with the children to make flowers. You could use:

cardboard circles
paper petals
glue
pipe cleaners

When each child has made a flower, sit down close together in a circle.

Have each child put her flower down in front of her.

One by one have the children twist the bottom of the stem around the top of the stem of the person to their left, ending with your own. With yours, connect the two ends of the circle.

continued

Project

Project

Closure with the Teacher Who's Leaving
(continued)

Say something to the effect, "This is a flower wreath that shows how glad we are for our times together." Hang the wreath on the wall. Be sure to tell the new teacher so the significance can be honored for a while after your parting.

A simple ceremony such as this can provide closure for your time with the children. Acknowledging what has been is essential for helping children to move on.

Project

Books to Pass on from Old Teacher to New

Using premade books, let each child dictate what the child wants the new teacher to know. The child draws or colors while the teacher who is leaving labels the pages for the new teacher. For example:

favorite color
who's in my family
favorite animal
what I especially like for snacks
my latest outdoor accomplishment (riding the trike, kicking a ball, crossing the monkey bars, etc.)

As the parting teacher helps make the books, he naturally reminisces with each child. Then the teacher who's leaving passes the books on to the new teacher, who also reads the books with the children, providing continuity as well as some hints into each child's needs and personality.

The "Knock, Knock, Knock" Game

Note:

Remind the children that it's OK to join in this game since their parents or guardians have already brought them to their school or child care center. Stress that they must *never* play a game like this, or any other game, with someone they don't know. If ever someone they do know comes to their home to play a game, tell the children they must get their parent or guardian's permission before they play.

Designate an area (the playground area around the tires, this half of the gym, or whatever works in your setting).

The children may find a place to "live" anywhere in that area. They have until you count to five to find their home.

Then go randomly from one to another.

At the first child, go around to her back. Say out loud,

"I'm gathering my friends,

1, 2, 3, 4.

Is _____ (that child's name) at home?

I'll knock on the door."

Say "Knock, knock, knock" while lightly tapping on child's back.

The child turns around.

Teacher says: "Hi, _____!" (that child's name)

Child says: "Hi, Sparky. _____ (Ms. Powell, or whatever you go by.)

Teacher says: "Come to (the name of your school or child care center) _____ with us."

Then that child goes around behind you and follows you to the next child. As the game goes on, the children can help you say the words. Change the ditty from "I'm gathering. . ." to "We're gathering. . . ."

When all the children are gathered, lead them in a circle, then circle them around to sit down.

This provides you an opportunity to talk with the children about your leaving.

If you happened to have the new teacher present, the departing teacher could gather the children while the new teacher watched (and listened, placing names to faces). Bringing the children together in a circle would provide a great opportunity for introducing the new teacher. You could then sing some of your favorite songs or otherwise transition from old to new.

Winger on Saying Goodbye to Teachers

I had a teacher when I was little. She let me make mud pies. I remember. We made dandelion cakes too. You know. Pretend. And we painted in pudding. And in the winter she pulled us on a sled. I remember.

But I don't remember saying goodbye to her. I think I didn't get to say goodbye. I liked her an awful lot. It would've been good to say goodbye.

Weaver Finch on Saying Goodbye

Note:
Use this story as a follow-up to your telling the children that you are leaving. Don't use it as the means for telling them. It is better that they hear news that might be distressing straight from you. The story will merely help ease the leaving.

Come gather round and I'll tell you a story.

Once, in a time very much like now, there was a child caregiver (teacher, or whatever your role is). She loved being with the children in _____ (name of your school or center). The children in her school were named _____, _____, etc. (the children's names). She remembered taking them on a walk and falling in the big pile of leaves. She remembered _____ (Help children recall memories. If needed, spark their recall with reminders of the weather, like "When it snowed. . . .").

But things changed and she couldn't be their teacher (caregiver, or . . .) anymore. Soon the children would have a new teacher (caregiver). His name is _____. He has _____ (color hair). His favorite color is _____. (His favorite animal, food to eat, etc.) He would have new ideas of fun things to do at school. The children wouldn't have to forget their old teacher. They would just get to have a new teacher too.

Finch, three, two, one. This story is done.

Terminal Illness in the Family

Note:
Grieving through a serious illness is a private family process, but one that needs to be acknowledged and accepted as a part of the child's life. We cannot, and should not, try to protect the child from the situation. We can, and should, give the family our support for the child going through the process.

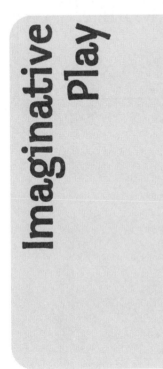

Illness

A doctor kit is essential. It allows the child to work with his deep fears. You may want to set up a hospital area. Without one, expect that the child may try to doctor in the middle of the block area. Alternately, some children may feel it's not okay to play about the illness. Perhaps they've been told not to in some other setting. Then they are likely to feel the need to hide the play. You'll want to invite that child to doctor or nurse all he wants as part of normal play.

If the child's loved one dies, be sure to keep the doctoring equipment available for weeks, even months afterwards. Then, more than ever, the child needs to be allowed to "play" about the events in her life. In play the child moves through feelings of anger, sadness, helplessness, abandonment, etc. And surrounded by real, alive children, the child's survival instincts will be nurtured through the interactive play.

The Importance of Small Things

Have little premade books available for the child to draw and dictate into, recording feelings, events, and accomplishments to give to the person who is ill.

Be careful not to push the child. The child will know exactly what suits him, and what will or will not be welcome by the family member who is ill.

Acknowledge and Offer Projects for Feelings

Be sure you sit face to face and let the child hear that you know her mom, dad, or whomever is very sick. Follow the child's lead, in whether to talk or not. Once you have acknowledged your awareness, then at least a door is open for the child to come to you, when and if she needs.

In the meantime, go on providing many tactile experiences to let the body move and let the feelings out. Examples:

water play

play dough

clay work

paper dough

Don't be concerned about the child making a product necessarily. Accept her actions when she smashes what she's made as much as you do when she wants to wrap up her creation as a gift for the sick person. What matters most is the child's process. Being there to support that process does help the child and the child's family. Remember, what they will most likely experience in the world is a shrinking back from people they know, almost as if death is contagious. Just being there will mean a lot to the family.

Winger on Serious Illness

Note:
Use this one-on-one with the child.

I guess I never told you, a couple of years ago my sister was very sick. She'd cough a whole lot, and sometimes throw up. You know how that sounds? When I was with her, I'd almost throw up too. Then at night sometimes, we'd cry together.

A couple of times she had to be rushed to the hospital. (Continue, if the child has already lost the loved one. Do not suggest imminent death unless the child brings it up as a possibility for her family. Occasionally, an adult in the family will share that death is being openly discussed, in which case you can too, individually with the child. Follow the child and family's lead in this regard.) The last time my sister went to the hospital she was too sick. There wasn't anything the doctors could do. I wasn't there when she died. But Mom was. It felt bad for a long, long time. Even now when I think about my sister, I still cry sometimes.

I heard your _____ is very sick. I wondered what it's like for you. _____ (response, or not).

Parent Traveling

Game for the Parent's Return

The child can help you set up a guessing game during the time that the parent is away. Use a paper bag or a shoe box. Towards the end of each day, let the child put one item into the bag. It might be one building block (not the whole set), or a piece of the particular yarn that was used in a project.

When the parent returns, invite him to come to your school or child care center and spend a few minutes with the child. The parent draws one item out of the bag at a time, and guesses what it was that the child did that day. At the end, the parent can help the child return the items to their places in the room, strengthening the connectedness between the parent and school.

Swinging and Tossing

A child whose parent travels a lot may have anger brewing. With these activities in the back of your mind, you can help diffuse anger on the spot. The swinging and striking arm motions in particular help move pent up anger through the body. Directed, the energy can be used in positive large muscle development, rather than being taken out on other children.

Newspaper Golf

Let children roll up several sheets of newspaper, which they tape into a "stick."

The child also wads up a smaller piece of newspaper into a ball. Rather than having holes in the ground for this form of "golf," make a starting line. Then pound in a stake across the field.

The children have to hit their "ball" across the field and bonk it into the stake. If you have toddlers who might fall on a stake, set out a string circle as the end goal.

Ringbee

You'll find directions for making ringbees in "To the Park."

The children can sail these into the air outdoors, without hurting anyone.

Variation: Try to land the ringbee in a cardboard box.

Travel

suitcase
briefcase
map
postcard
plane or train ticket
telephone

Winger and Feelings of Missing a Parent

Sometimes if a child is allowed to exaggerate a feeling, the actual feeling diminishes. Puppet Winger can help with this.

Use Winger to voice the child's feelings, and allow the child to repeat after him. Since it's imaginary friend Winger talking, the child won't feel her feelings are being belittled.

Example: Winger says, "I miss my mom! Whaa! Whaa!" (or whatever you've heard the child express at some earlier time).

Simply allowing the children to go "Whaa! Whaa!" validates their feeling. They may, in fun, rub their eyes and pretend to cry. They will know that you know how they feel, and hopefully won't have to "act out" in some more difficult-to-read way.

Skippety on Mommy Traveling

Sometimes when
my mommy's away
I just want her home
with me, to play.
Just her and me
climbing a tree,
Or the two of us
riding a bus.
Or Mommy and I
making a delicious, gooey, super chewy
chocolate pie!
When mommy's away
I'm sad through the day.
Sometimes I'm sad
through a whole night *and* day.

Tumultuous Times

Unfortunately we cannot control such scary situations as terrorism, school violence, random shootings, or bombings. We can't even predict what form these horrors might take. Since we cannot predict violent acts, we cannot plan for them. Certainly, if we could plan around them, we would have our children at a distance, well-protected. Since that's not the nature of such events, and since we cannot guarantee that our children won't be involved or otherwise affected by random acts of violence or intentional terrorism, we need to make plans for what we can do to help our children feel safe and secure when they're in our care. We can keep calming and nurturing activities in mind in case our children become privy to such acts. Remember that children need not be directly present to be deeply affected.

 Should we find ourselves in the midst of a tumultuous situation, immediate safety must be of first concern. Now is the time to review your emergency procedures. Alert volunteers to the guidelines so everyone is up-to-date.

If something does happen nearby, or even if something happens at a great distance but our children arrive at school or child care having heard of the occurrence, we must immediately reassure the children that we are there to protect them. Comfort the children first. Hold them. Answer questions simply and directly. Children do not need to know all that we know, but if they come to us having heard of an event, their awareness needs to be acknowledged. We might say, "Tell me what you've heard. Tell me what's upsetting." Then follow up with reassurance or gentle realignment of their understanding of the facts. Children may have the situation way out of proportion to what has actually happened. It's tricky in group settings to respond to the precocious child without alarming the oblivious ones. You will know, based on your close relationship with the children, whether to talk with them as a group or whether to take advantage of individual moments together to answer questions and reassure.

Do not allow TV coverage to be played in the children's presence. This is an absolute. You cannot know what scene might be shown next. Furthermore, do not talk with other adults about a horrific event in front of the children, especially if the adults are likely to recount the specific details, ad infinitum. Your more experienced volunteers can assist new helpers in understanding the importance of this emotional protection. Encourage parents and guardians to watch or listen to the news only at times and in places separate from their young children.

Activities to Calm the Children

After acknowledging the event, we can offer whatever activities we deem needed to help the children feel calmed and nurtured. Here are some ideas for immediate response to tumultuous times:

Repeat any activity in this book that you have noticed soothed the children.

Invite the children to be held and rocked.

Sing lullabies together.

Read their favorite books. Reread them as often as the children request.

Play peaceful music.

Provide warm water play.

Offer playdough.

Have drawing materials readily available. Children will express their inner fears through pictures, giving you the opportunity to talk with them about what they have drawn.

Encourage home-corner play with baby care, all the while observing their actions. The children will take care of others, just as they want to be taken care of.

Introduce a teddy bear or stuffed animal day, when all the children bring a soft toy from home. Let the children set up special sleeping and eating areas for their "friends." Cheerios served on a miniature china tea set suit the teddy bears as well as their owners. After snacks the children can read to their animals and put them to bed. As the children nurture their teddy bear, they are comforting themselves.

Imaginative Play

Response to a Tumultuous Event

Add medics, firefighters, police hats, or props to the home-corner equipment, as fits the situation. For instance, place rubber gloves and an anthrax scanning machine (a box with open ends) that the mail has to pass through, in the imaginary play section, if your children have been affected by postal terrorism. Children need to play their way through the events. As I've mentioned previously, don't be alarmed if a child who has lost someone close plays out the occurrence over and over. Through play, the child and his friends will come to terms with their fears and loss.

Activity

Large Muscle Movements

A second phase of helping children move angry, fearful, or sad feelings through them may become necessary in a day or two. Encourage these large muscle activities as soon as the children have had time to adjust to the initial shock:

Repeat any of the activities in this book that use a swinging or pounding motion.

Encourage children to ride big wheels in outdoor playtime.

Use your creative movement music to jump, hop, skip, run with the children.

Do stretching exercises, which will help release stuck feelings.

Be sure to have a safe spot, a cozy place for children to retreat if they need to. Allow blankies from home during any traumatic time, even if you normally don't.

Do keep to your daily routines, as that will comfort the children. Suspend any difficult projects, plans, field trips, or activities though, to allow for more of these nurturing activities, which can soothe children through the difficult time.

Family Violence

Project

Molding

Let the child tear a paper egg carton in bits.

Soak paper bits in water, overnight.

Add a little warm water. Let child squish, squeeze, splat, mold.

Mixture can be saved for second or third day's use, adding more water if it becomes too thick.

You can also offer this activity in the water table, adding plastic figures or other objects related to the child's distress.

Activity

Soothing a Pet

Put on soothing music.

Bring out a toy dog. Sit down near the affected child and start brushing the dog's hair with a small brush.

Ruffle up the dog's hair. Ask it, "Are you my rumpled pet?" Then go back to brushing.

Depending on your relationship with the child, you might wait until the child asks for a turn (shouldn't be long), or ask, "Would you help me smooth my rumpled pet?"

A Chance for Control (one or two children at a time)

Note: This activity is only suitable for children who *will not* put items into their mouths.

Set about 20 marbles out on a table in front of one or two affected children. Of course the marbles might roll. And the child might get frustrated.

Putter nearby until it seems the child will be open to something more.

Follow up with blobs of colored clay. Plop blobs down on the table. You might not want to say anything, or you may want to simply offer, "Try this."

The children will gain control by poking the marbles into the clay. If they seem unsure of what they are "supposed" to do, tell the children they can make anything they want with the marbles and clay. They will feel what they need to.

Allow the child(ren) to play as long as they want, poking marbles in the clay.

Follow up:

Collect most of the clay. Set out a basin of warm water. Let the children wash the marbles and dry on a cookie rack, covered with paper towels.

Orange Juice

Using an old-fashioned juicing boat, let child rub, rub, back and forth, to squeeze oranges into juice. Serve in the smallest cups available, so the child is able to squeeze enough for everyone. The rhythmic twisting of the arm and shoulders will work feelings out of the child's body. The child will be positively, appreciatively involved. And the Vitamin C can only help a child with an assaulted immune system.

Activity

Outdoor Games

Any throwing movement that uses overhand lob or underhand swing, helps to move stuck feelings of anger and resentment through a child. Remember, a child who lives with violence, learns the behavior she sees. We can provide positive ways to move the aggressive feelings through a child, so she doesn't become violent too.

Basketball: A spontaneous game of basketball, using a wastebasket or open paper bag for a basket, a soft rubber ball or a wad of newspaper will help aggression move through a child.

Hockey: Again, the ball can be a wadded sheet of newspaper, the stick, a rolled and taped half of paper bag.

Weaver Finch on Family Arguments

Come gather round and I'll tell you a story.

Once there were two children lonely for parents who had time for hugs. The first thing the children heard in the morning was yelling and slamming of doors. The last thing the children usually heard at night was crying and slamming of doors. The children hugged each other, but they often felt hurting and sad.

One morning though, very, very early, the younger child heard a tap tap tapping on their little bitty window. He shook his older sister, because at first the boy was afraid. It was only barely light outside.

Once wakened, the girl was wide awake. The house was very quiet. It was a lovely still quiet. Just as the little boy was pointing to the window, a bird's head popped up from the ledge outside. "Tap, tap, tap," it knocked on the pane again.

The little boy and the bigger girl were delighted. Slowly they scooted to the end of their bed to get a closer look at their visitor. The bird had a black cap and bright eyes.

Weaver Finch on Family Arguments
(continued)

The little bird became the children's friend. Every night when they went to bed, the thought of the bird coming in the morning took their minds off the yelling. And every morning they woke early, to that lovely quiet. They didn't want to miss a single tap, tap, tap.

Some mornings the little bird was at the window. Some mornings it wasn't, but there was always a cloud to watch, or rain on the window pane, or a spider working on a web. The children didn't feel nearly as sad as they had before the little boy heard the bird's first tap, tap, tapping.

Finch, three, two, one. This story is done.

In Closing

The children. Many will come booming through your door, ready to grab these ideas, adding unique twists of their own as imaginations gallop. There will be other children who hang back, who watch and listen and soak in; these children especially need acknowledgements of their inner lives. Then there may be more careful, thoughtful children who mull over what's presented, turning collections of materials into works of art. There may also be the butterfly children, the ever-moving fluttering ones who take bits of whatever is offered with a happy give and take. Each group in your care will be distinctive. Each group will use the activities in their own way, sometimes as singular experiences, other times interweaving the activities as part of the group myth.

The children come first. Trust what you know about each group of children. Your attentiveness to their interests, concerns, perspectives will make these activities fit most precisely to their needs. Every one of the steps in the activities could be accompanied with a teacher's asking the children, "What do you think?" When it comes to topics that arise from their inner lives, the children will know what suits them.

Finally, your memories, your recollections of what it was to be a child, your own intuition will breathe life into these endeavors. Your enthusiasm and excitement for being and doing with the children gives validation to their life energy.

Enjoy. And don't be afraid when the children are in pain, or when they're scared or angry. If acknowledged, those feelings fly off as seed fluffs on the wind. Over time, you will be giving their core inclinations—towards health and growth and happiness—room to flourish. Individualizing your curriculum means embracing the children, and their burgeoning love of life. Again, enjoy.

Appendix

Recycled Materials to Have on Hand

paper egg cartons
small boxes, from jewelry boxes to tissue
  and cereal boxes
toilet paper, paper towel, and wrapping
  paper tubes
plastic spice containers
baking powder cans and lids
scrap wood
grab bag or box
large cardboard box
a few sheets of thin cardboard, such as
  from department store
clothing boxes
newspaper
paper bags
fabric scraps
wrapping paper

Supplies to Have on Hand

toothpicks
poster paint
plastic tubing
popsicle sticks
liquid starch
soap flakes (not granules)
stamped postcards, ready to address
  and mail
food coloring
masking tape
glue
construction paper
cotton balls
straws
pipe cleaners

Expand on the Topics with Flannel Board Activities

Earlier I mentioned that inanimate friends can speak for the child. So, too, can flannel board activities provide a means through which the child expresses her reality. It's much easier for a child to tell you a story as he places felt pieces up on a flannel board than it is to talk with you directly about feelings. Children will tell their own stories. They will also use the felt pieces to recreate their life experience, as a way of gaining some control over unsatisfactory situations.

In order to keep the cost of this book affordable for all early childhood educators and caregivers, we made the tough decision not to include felt patterns for flannel board activities in the text. I would encourage you to find artistic volunteers among your parents, grandparents, even your children's siblings. Ask your artistic volunteer to draw simple outlines that can then be cut out of scraps of felt. No details are necessary. The only requirement is that the objects be recognizable. Using simple outlines also encourages the children's imaginations.

 For more variety, or if you cannot find someone in your community who has the time or ability to draw, you can use pictures cut out of magazines for the story pieces, with flannel backing glued on.

The children place the felt pieces on the front of a board covered with flannel or even on a blanket stretched over a pillow. The story-telling activity can be offered for individual use or with a partner at free choice time.

Following you will find some suggestions for felt pieces. This is by no means an exhaustive list. Flannel board sets can be created around any topic, especially those about which the children may have pent-up feelings.

Basic Set:
figures that can be used as family or community members
vehicles
homes of various sizes and types (small house, large house, apartment building, mobile home, etc.)
trees and shrubs

Here are some ideas for adding to the Family Play Section.

Car Trip:

car	city building	lake
sport utility vehicle	house	river
delivery truck	mobile home	trees
pickup truck	barn	

Pond Life:

pond	frog	turtle
dragonfly	tadpole	cattail
duck	fish	
log	lily pad	

Oak Woods:

owl	oak tree
rock	acorn
squirrel	oak leaf
blue jay	yellow wood violet

For your interest, these items show interdependence in nature. The tree provides food for the animals and birds. The yellow wood violet only grows in acid soil such as created by the trees' decaying leaves.

Just about any topic in the Changes section can be expanded with flannel board activities. Try adding these to your packets.

Weather:

rainbow	clouds	snowflake
sun	raindrops	wind

Cold Weather Clothing:

winter clothing to put on children from the Basic Set

coat	scarf
warm pants	mittens
hood	boots

Firefighting:

fire truck	ax
hose	fire fighter
coupling	smoke
hydrant	flames

Use buildings and trees from your Basic Set.

Encourage the child to tell you the story that she has made with the flannel pieces. It may be easier for a child to tell a story, than to talk directly about having been involved in a fire.

Moving:

car and trailer	bus	ferry
moving van	airplane	

Use buildings and people from the Basic Set.

The child will choose those that apply to his family.

Let the child tell you the story of the departure, including where the friend or sibling will be living next, and how they will stay in touch.

Illness:

patient	pillow	stethoscope	cloud
family	blanket	sun	raindrops
bed	window		

Doctor or other health care providers can be from the Basic Set.

Winger Puppet Pattern

 You may have a parent or volunteer who is handy at sewing. If so, perhaps that person will make the class a Winger puppet.

Winger Puppet Pattern Instructions

1. Select fabric for pattern pieces. The hands and "W" work best cut out of felt. The head can be a corresponding skin color. Choose contrasting colors for the shirt and "W."
2. Fold all fabric in half so that you cut 2 identical pieces of each pattern (except the "W").
3. Pin pattern pieces on selected fabrics. Cut out all pieces along outer lines.
4. On the outside of one of the head pieces, embroider or use fabric marker for Winger's facial features and hair.
5. Stitch or glue the "W" on the outside of the shirt front.

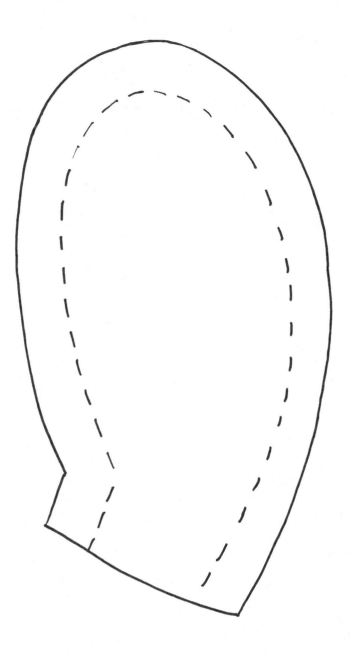

6. If you are not using felt for the hands, cut a small amount of batting, big enough to fit in the palms of the hands. Slip the palm stuffing in between each set of hands and stitch each hand together, from the outside. For felt hands, which will be thick enough in themselves, simply stitch together.

7. Out of a stiffening material, cut two pieces the size of the wings and one piece the size of the head. Baste the stiffener onto the inside of each wing and on the inside of the head back.

8. Place the insides of two wings and the face piece onto the inside front of the shirt (the one with the "W"), with the shirt upright and the other three pieces facing down. The *insides* of the three pieces will face the *inside* of the shirt. You should have all narrow edges at the top. Pin along the top edge only. Do the same placing and pinning with the back set.

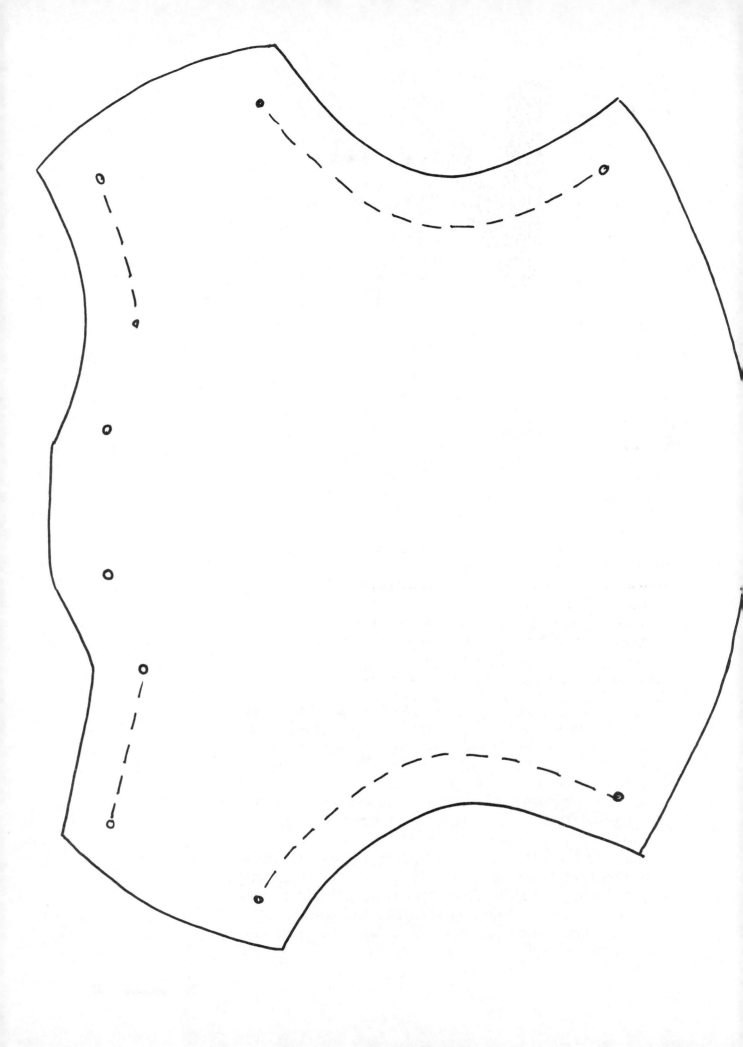

9. Flip the wing and head pieces up. Match front and back of entire sets with the outsides of both sets touching. Pin around the edges of the wings and the head.

10. Carefully, one by one, sew around the wing and head pieces, matching notches, leaving openings at the neck for the fingers to go through. (Do not sew along the top of the neck. You will manipulate the puppet with the middle finger in the head and the ring and index fingers in the wings.)

11. Sew the shirt together, leaving unstitched all areas between dots: at the top, bottom, and sleeve ends. Carefully clip curve under arm.

12. Turn all pieces right side out. The two wings and head should now appear upright along the top of the shirt.

13. Turn the sleeves under at the cuff and slip the hands into sleeves, being careful to position the thumbs up. Pin the hands in place in the sleeves. Top stitch to hold in place.

14. Hand stitch in between the three finger openings, if need be, to close any holes between the finger openings.

15. Machine hem bottom of shirt.

Song Sheets

Pebble Song

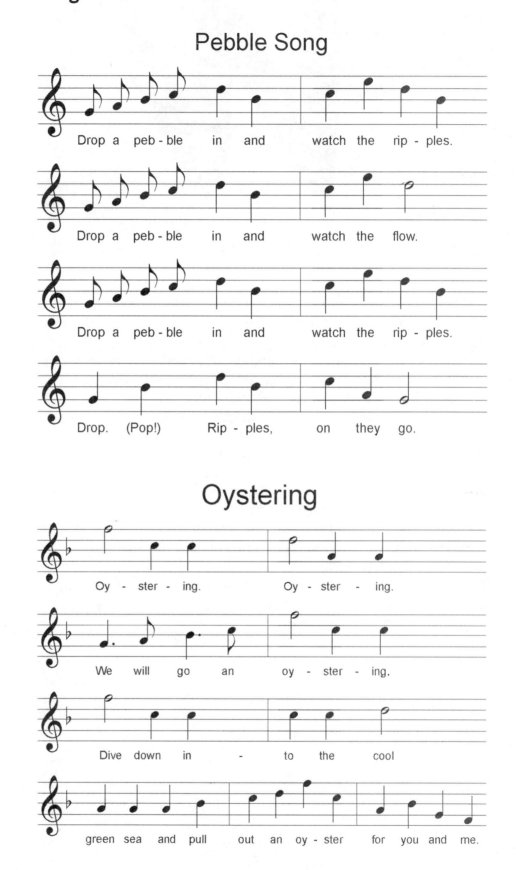

Oystering

Premade Books

Ask volunteers to make up a number of books to have on hand for follow-up individualizing with the children. To make the books, simply cut pages (such as half of standard 8.5 × 11-inch paper) and staple together on the left side. The books can be of various sizes, with and without simple construction paper covers.

Home Involvement

Winger Puppet

Offer a Winger puppet for families to check out and take home over the weekend.

Copy the pattern for families to make their own Winger.

Flannel Board Pieces

Label flannel board packets according to topic.

Offer the sets for families to check out for home use.

Songs

Send home the song sheets to interested families and invite them in to share their rendition.